研究生
学术英语
系列教材

总主编 **王永祥**

夏晓蓉 编著

Academic Spoken English

学术英语口语教程

清华大学出版社
北 京

内 容 简 介

教材共 12 章,旨在循序渐进、全面系统地训练学生的学术英语口语能力,培养学生参加国际学术会议、用英语做学术演讲的能力,从而提升其学术思维能力。本教材的口语练习涉及的话题广泛,有助于学生对话题做进一步的深入研究,并以英语演讲的方式来阐述多元化观点。本教材配套的音视频和阅读材料以及 PPT 课件资源,读者可通过扫描正文相应的二维码进行学习,也可通过点击 https://pan.baidu.com/s/1Sgl8fKv6Guj1snd6rjFVSA(提取码:v7f9)下载使用。

本教材既可作为我国高校研究生和高年级本科生的学术英语教材,又可供有兴趣提高学术英语口语能力的学生作为课后辅导教材使用。

图书在版编目(CIP)数据

学术英语口语教程 / 王永祥总主编;夏晓蓉编著. —北京:清华大学出版社,2019(2024.6 重印)
(研究生学术英语系列教材)
ISBN 978-7-302-53153-1

Ⅰ. ①学… Ⅱ. ①王… ②夏… Ⅲ. ①英语—口语—研究生—教材 Ⅳ. ① H319.9

中国版本图书馆 CIP 数据核字(2019)第 114419 号

责任编辑:刘 艳
封面设计:子 一
责任校对:王凤芝
责任印制:丛怀宇

出版发行:清华大学出版社
   网 址:https://www.tup.com.cn, https://www.wqxuetang.com
   地 址:北京清华大学学研大厦 A 座   邮 编:100084
   社 总 机:010-83470000   邮 购:010-62786544
   投稿与读者服务:010-62776969, c-service@tup.tsinghua.edu.cn
   质量反馈:010-62772015, zhiliang@tup.tsinghua.edu.cn
印 装 者:涿州市般润文化传播有限公司
经 销:全国新华书店
开 本:185mm×260mm   印 张:9.5   字 数:210 千字
版 次:2019 年 7 月第 1 版   印 次:2024 年 6 月第 7 次印刷
定 价:48.00 元

产品编号:082252-01

总　序

国际著名应用语言学家肯·海兰德（Ken Hyland）在其所著《学术用途英语：高级资源全书》（*English for Academic Purposes: An Advanced Resource Book*，2006）一书的前言中将学术英语（English for Academic Purposes）定义为"旨在帮助学习者以英语进行学习或研究的英语教学活动（teaching English with the aim of assisting learners' study or research in that language）"。

最近十多年来，学术英语已然成为英语教学与研究领域的焦点之一；而在非英语专业研究生的英语教学中，学术英语的重要性尤为突出。研究生教育处于整个教育链之最高端，尽管各高校对研究生培养目标的表述有异，但都必然包含科学研究能力的要求。"研究生"一词中的"研"字本义是"细磨与深入地探求"，非常清晰地凸显了研究生教育的首要任务：培养研究生的学术研究能力。非英语专业研究生在进行其本专业学术研究的过程中，不可避免地需要阅读大量外语（主要是英语）文献，需要出国访学或深造，需要参加国际学术会议。在高等教育日益国际化的今天，研究生教育肩负着培养高素质国际化人才的使命。英语作为一门世界通用的语言，在研究生教育中发挥着越来越重要的作用。

在此背景下，通识英语课程已经无法满足学术交流日益国际化的专业培养需求。自2016年起，南京师范大学根据学校"十三五"规划和"创建有国际影响力高水平大学"的办学目标，在既有的分层教学改革基础上进行反复调研和论证，开始了新一轮基于国际化学术能力提升的研究生公共英语教学改革。该教学改革首先在两个学院试点，对其硕士研究生开设学术英语系列课程（包括"学术英语口语""国际学术交流英语""学术英语写作""学术英语翻译"等），着重培养研究生独立撰写英语论文、参与英语学术讲座和国际学术会议的能力，使他们率先具备良好的国际视野。2017年，这项教学改革逐步推广至更多学院，也得到校领导和校研究生院的大力支持。通过改革，我们已经形成一套成熟的非英语专业硕士研究生学术英语课程体系，所开设课程受到试点学院研究生的认可和好评，也引起校内外同行的关注。有鉴于此，我们组建了长期从事非英语专业研究生英语教学实践并直接参与本轮教学改革的教师团队，认真总结本轮教学改革中的教学经验，大量阅读国内外先进的学术英语论著，编写了本套研究生学术英语教材，共四本。它们分别是：《学术英语口语教程》《国际学术交流英语》《学术英语写作教程》和《学术英语翻译教程》。

《学术英语口语教程》旨在循序渐进、全面系统地训练学生的学术英语口语能力，培养学生参加学术会议、用英语做学术演讲的能力，从而提升其学术思维能力。

《国际学术交流英语》以参加国际学术会议为主线，内容涉及国际学术会议的信息来源、会议通信、论文提交、经济资助、会议主持、演讲、讨论、会议海报和与专业人士交谈等，选材具有时代性、规范性、全面性、知识性和启迪性，便于学生获取信息和提高学术交流能力。

　　《学术英语写作教程》基于过程性写作理念，详细介绍学术写作之准备过程、写作步骤及后续工作，帮助学生熟悉学术写作流程。该教材秉持学术英语写作文体的特殊性，重点介绍学术论文写作的文体风格，以步骤和阶段思想介绍学术论文各部分写作的内容要点和行文规范。同时，该教材还提供了丰富的例句表达，供学生参考使用。

　　《学术英语翻译教程》着重帮助学生系统掌握英汉学术语篇互译的基本理论与技巧，培养学生英汉学术语篇差异意识，并在选例上与学生的专业相结合，使其在学习英汉互译的基本理论和技巧时，夯实其专业英语知识，最终提高其国际学术交流能力。

　　我校基于国际化学术能力提升的研究生公共英语教学改革仍在路上；摆在读者面前的这套学术英语系列教材必将助力研究生公共英语教学改革。我们深知，改革没有尽头，有的仅是一个又一个新的起点，唯有不断改革方能让教育返璞归真。我们期待亲爱的读者在使用本套教材的过程中提出宝贵建议，期待各位同仁在今后的研究生公共英语教学改革中结出累累硕果，期待全体研究生在这场教学改革中真正提升自己的国际学术交流能力！

　　在本套教材编写的过程中，南京师范大学研究生院领导和外国语学院领导给予了大力支持，清华大学出版社同仁也给我们提出了宝贵意见，在此，我们全体编者对他们的帮助致以最衷心的感谢！

南京师范大学　王永祥

2019 年 2 月 28 日于秦淮河畔小屋

前　言

为了提高在全球化背景下的竞争力，中国需要培养出更多具有国际视野、通晓国际规则、能够参与国际事务和国际竞争的人才。具备专业知识的大学生和研究生越来越需要通过英语来帮助他们适应国际化的需求。除了能用英语查找和阅读专业资料外，他们还希望能更多地参与以英语为工作语言的专业讲座和会议，能在会议上宣读论文和参与讨论，能充分利用国家提供的基金项目去国外参加短期或长期的科研活动。在专业学习和进修中用英语表达个人学术观点，能与他人讨论学术问题，展现学术能力，发出中国学术的声音，这是当前很多学生学习英语的目的。本教材正是为了适应这种需求而编写的。

本教材旨在对学生进行循序渐进、全面系统的学术英语口语能力的训练。学生不仅能学习学术英语演讲的主要技能，掌握参加学术研讨会所需的技巧，还能进行学术思维能力的训练。本教材共有 12 章。第 1 章引导学生进入不同的学术场景。第 2 章和第 3 章通过口语练习展示如何在演讲中吸引、引导听众，如何有逻辑地展开观点，以及如何在结束部分给听众留下深刻印象。第 4 章针对学术英语演讲的技巧进行口语训练。第 5 章通过三种学术活动让学生充分练习第 2 章至第 4 章学到的学术英语演讲技能。除了学会表达自己的学术观点外，学生还需要学会聆听其他研究者的观点，并与他们进行交流。因此，第 6、8、9 和第 10 章主要培养学生听懂学术讲座、了解学术研讨会、主持学术研讨会以及在不同的学术活动中提问与回答的能力。第 7 章和第 11 章主要训练学生的学术思维能力，包括用何种方式阐述观点、从何种角度思考问题、如何进行批判性思维和辩论等。第 12 章设计了三个研讨会，可供教师考察或测试学生所学的学术英语口语技能。

本教材口语练习涉及的话题广泛，无论是人工智能、全球变暖、基因工程等与科技发展相关的话题，还是高等教育、网上支付、二胎政策等与社会发展相关的话题，都是学生比较熟悉和感兴趣的。另外，本教材还提供了相关的音视频和阅读材料，有助于学生对话题做进一步的研究，了解同一话题的不同看法，并获取信息来支持自己的观点，这也是学术活动的重要环节之一。学生可通过扫描正文相应的二维码进行学习，也可通过访问"内容简介"里的网盘链接进行下载使用。

在讨论各类话题时，对于比较熟悉的话题，学生或独立思考，或与他人合作；而对于不太熟悉的话题，学生可以通过相关音视频和阅读材料获取更多的信息，从而形成多元化的观点，并进行充分讨论。这些信息也能成为学生论证自身观点的依据。通过不同的方式来阐述自身观点是培养学生学术英语口语能力的基础。在此基础之上，学生可以运用各种英语演讲技巧来充分展示自己的学术能力。

本教材是学术英语教学试点小组集体智慧的结晶。在编写过程中，我们查阅了大量国内外学术英语口语教学的理论和实践资料，引入了网络和书本的各类信息，从国内外学者身上得到了各类启示，在此谨向他们表示衷心的感谢。同时也向为本教材的编写提供反馈和修改意见的清华大学出版社编辑表示衷心的感谢。

最后，由于编者水平和经验有限，教材中难免有不足之处，欢迎广大师生随时给我们提出宝贵意见和建议。衷心祝愿各院校的老师和学生不断取得教与学的新成果！

编者

2019 年 3 月

Contents

Contents

1 Chapter

Speaking Academically

Warm-up Questions:

1. Have you had any experience of classroom presentation in English?

2. If you want to go to international academic conferences, how will you get access to the conference notices?

3. What is a seminar? Have you attended any seminars?

With the remarkable economic development of China, Chinese students have increasing access to international communication and cooperation, either by studying abroad, or by participating in some short-term international programs, like international academic conferences or exchange study. Are you ready to speak English in different academic situations?

Section 1 / **Academic Situations**

1.1 Look at the academic situations below. Then fulfill the tasks.

- Giving a formal presentation in class;
- Discussing and giving your opinion in a seminar on preassigned reading materials;
- Discussing with your tutor in one-to-one tutorial (e.g. about your preliminary report or paper writing plan);
- Presenting yourself and answering questions during your thesis defense.

_____

_____

_____

_____

_____

1. Discuss with your partner to extend the list.

2. If you have had any academic experience, describe it in detail. Your description should include the following aspects:

   - Where did you have the experience?
   - Who were the participants and how many of them?
   - How much time was assigned to each participant?
   - What was the purpose?
   - How did you perform in that situation?

1.2 Look at the two pictures below. Then fulfill the tasks.

1. Discuss with your partner about the differences between a lecture and a seminar.

2. Tell your opinion to other students in class.

3. Try to argue with your partner which has more advantages, a lecture or a seminar. You have to take an opposite stance.

4. After the argument, make a summary of the advantages and disadvantages respectively in the chart below.

	Advantages	Disadvantages
Lecture		
Seminar		

1.3 Read the following paragraph. Work with your partner to identify the differences between a tutorial and a seminar. Remember to use your own words.

A tutorial is usually for a small number of students, say, between two and five, whereas a seminar is attended by a larger group, say, between ten and fifteen. In a tutorial, a tutor adopts the role of the expert and asks and answers questions related to his most recent lectures. Often a student has to submit an essay or a report which is discussed by the tutor and then by other members of the tutorial group. In short, the tutor takes the lead; he in fact "tutors". The purpose of the seminar, however, is to provide an opportunity to discuss a previously arranged topic. More than one member of the staff might be present and one of them would probably act as chairman. Often one student gives a short talk served as an introduction to the discussion. Other students may have been asked to read a number of chapters of a book, related to the talk, so as to be well-prepared to participate in the discussion.

Section 2
International Academic Programs

2.1 Read the following notice from a foreign university website. Then answer the questions below.

If you:
- Are currently attending one university and want to take York University courses with a letter of permission;
- Already hold an undergraduate degree from an accredited university or university-level institution;
- Do not hold an undergraduate degree from any university but want to enrol in York University courses to fulfill the academic upgrading or professional development requirements of a professional designation;
- Have a doctoral degree or equivalent professional training or experience at the time of application;
- Have sufficient proficiency in the English language to carry out the project required.

1. What are these qualifications for?

    _____

2. Have you applied for any international academic programs? If yes, what qualifications
    are required? If not, do you have some plans in the future?

    _____

    _____

    _____

2.2 Below is a notice from the website of MIT on applying for postdoctoral fellowship. Read the notice and discuss with your partner about the contents required in different letters.

> **How to Apply as a Postdoc**
>
> Please send the following information:
> - A letter describing the kind of work you would like to do at MIT and the particular research group or faculty member whose research interests coincide with your own. Also include the dates you would like to visit.
> - A curriculum vitae.
> - Three letters of recommendation.
> - At least one publication or writing sample.

2.3 If your application is accepted, the department will contact you with further details and paperwork about your visit. Discuss the following questions with your partner and simulate a conversation between the department and the applicant according to your answers to these questions.

1. What does the department want to know about you?
2. Do you have some questions for the department?

2.4 Read the following notice of a workshop and talk about the information you learn from it to your partner. Then fill in the form.

Ph.D. Placements and Supervisor Mobility Grants U.K. and China

About This Opportunity

The U.K.-China Joint Research and Innovation Partnership Fund (known in the U.K. as the Newton Fund) Ph.D. placement program is delivered by the British Council in China and the China Scholarship Council on behalf of the U.K.'s Department for Business, Innovation, and Skills and China's Ministry of Education respectively.

This program is a sponsorship opportunity for the U.K. and Chinese Ph.D. students and their supervisors to spend a period of study of three to twelve months (for Ph.D. students) and up to three months (for supervisors) at higher education institutions in China or the U.K. The focus is on research areas that reflect the common interests and demands of both countries, including:

- Health and life sciences;
- Food and water security;
- Environmental technologies;
- Energy;
- Urbanisation;
- Education and creative economy for economic development and social welfare.

Please note, applicants must find a host institution in their target country and placements must start between January and December 2017.

Eligibility

This opportunity is open to the U.K. and Chinese nationals who are currently enrolled, as Ph.D. students, at accredited higher education institutions or research institutions in the U.K. or China respectively. The U.K. students studying for their Ph.D.s at institutions in China and Chinese students studying for their Ph.D.s at institutions in the U.K. are not eligible.

The U.K. Ph.D. applicants should be from the U.K. institutions with strong research record in the six areas of focus mentioned above. The U.K. applicants should be the U.K. passport holders. Candidates of other nationalities must hold passports from countries that have diplomatic relations with China.

Host universities in China must be eligible to admit international students.

Deadline

The application process closes at 12:00 p.m. GMT on 20 September 2016.

Please visit the official program page (see British Council website) for more information about how to apply and documents to download.

Program	
Sponsor	
Duration	
Qualifications	
Themes	

2.5 Read the following questions and try to remember them. Then find the answers to them while watching the video about Asian leadership by Nicholas Tse.

1. Who is MC?

_____

_____

_____

2. What is the theme of the conference?

_____

_____

_____

3. Why is Nicholas Tse invited to talk to the students?

_____

_____

_____

4. How many sessions are there in this conference?

_____

_____

_____

5. Who presides the question and answer session?

_____

_____

_____

Extensive Reading

Visiting researcher scholars are individuals who possess a Ph.D. or its equivalent, and whose primary purpose for residence on the Berkeley campus is to conduct independent research. The length of stay for a visiting researcher scholar is at least one month and appointments are granted one year at a time, with a maximum cumulative appointment time of two years. Visiting researcher scholar positions are not compensated. However, units may provide a stipend of up to $10,000 per year. Such stipends can be used to cover things such as living expenses, travel costs, and incidental research expenses, but not as a form of salary compensation.

Visiting student researchers are applicants who are currently enrolled in a degree program and are working to obtain a degree. Generally, visiting student researchers must hold a minimum of a Bachelor's degree or its equivalent. Visiting student researcher positions are not compensated. However, units may provide a stipend of up to $10,000 per year. Such stipends can be used to cover things such as living expenses, travel costs, and incidental research expenses, but not as a form of salary compensation.

2 Chapter

Attracting Your Audience

Warm-up Questions:

1. In what situations will we give an oral presentation?

2. Have you delivered any presentations? What is your topic? Who are the audience?

3. If not, have you listened to other people's presentations? What do they talk about?

4. What are the differences between reading a paper and listening to an oral presentation?

It is necessary to deliver an oral presentation in many academic situations. How can we attract the audience at the beginning and impress them at the end? Some useful strategies like using interesting stories, provocative questions, and startling facts will make a desirable effect.

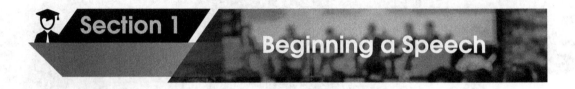

Section 1 Beginning a Speech

1.1 Look at the two pictures below and try to distinguish a presentation from a conversation with the keywords in the box.

intimate	friendly	formal	close
instant	far away	indifferent	casual

1. The relationship between the two guys in the conversation is _____ while that between the speaker and the audience is _____ .

2. The two guys in the conversation are _____ in terms of the distance. In contrast, the speaker and the audience are relatively _____ from each other.

1.2 Describe the differences in the two pictures in terms of "reaction", "atmosphere" and "use of words". You can imitate the expressions above.

1. _____

   _____

2. _____

_____

3. _____

_____

1.3 Watch the beginning part of the TED Talk "The Secrets of Spider Venom". Then answer the following questions.

1. How does the speaker attract listeners' attention? Is he successful?

_____

_____

2. What do most people think of spiders?

_____

_____

3. What is the speaker's view of spiders?

_____

_____

4. Think about what effect is produced when listeners know the speaker has a different idea from most people.

_____

_____

1.4 Discuss the question with your partner: What strategies can be used to effectively grab listeners' attention when you are giving a speech?

1.5 If you have no good idea, read the following examples. Then work with your partner to identify what strategies are used to lead the audience into the presentation in each example.

- **Example 1:** Good morning, ladies and gentlemen. I'd like to start my presentation with a question: What can ruin our life? (Encourage the audience to give answers: failure in career, family tragedy, loss of belief, fatal disease, etc.) But people say that if you want to ruin a child's life, just give him or her a smartphone. Many children, especially those left behind in the countryside, are addicted to games on smartphones. Today I'd like to report our survey into the effect of smartphones on children in Jiangsu Province.

- **Example 2:** "Sounds good my man, see ya soon, I'll tw…" This is the last message from Alexander Heit, a 22-year-old college student with good grades and a quick wit, who died from replying to a text message on his smartphone when he was driving. Last year, tragedies from using smartphones were heard again and again. Then shall we ban smartphones as a result? It is difficult. A better solution is to help people avoid dangers while using smartphones. Today I would like to introduce an app to warn people of dangers who get lost in smartphones.

- **Example 3:** Ladies and gentlemen, good morning! I am here to talk to you about a disease. Some of you may already be affected; most of you will in some way be touched by this disease. If this disease can't be eradicated, it will have a direct and serious impact on every person in this room!

- **Example 4:** Good afternoon, everyone! There is a Chinese saying "with a hare under one's garment" to describe the uneasiness for a nervous person. That is how I am feeling at such a moment, and before such a big audience, there seems to be a hare under my garment. Well, now speaking about "nervous", I would like to show you the result of my experiment on the nervous system of rabbits.（胡庚申，2013）

Examples	Strategies
1	
2	
3	
4	

Tips

Attention grabbers are techniques you use in the introduction of a speech as a means to hook your audience's attention and get them interested in your topic. They may also provide a pathway to your thesis statement of your presentation. Provoking questions, interesting stories, quotations, startling statements, and humors are common attention grabbers.

1.6 **Look at the contents in the box that might be used in the introduction part of a presentation. Then read the presentation below and match 1–8 with a–h in the box.**

a. self-introduction	b. greetings	c. attention grabbers
d. topic	e. general purpose	f. thesis statement
g. main points	h. question and answer plan	

Good afternoon, ladies and gentlemen.

My name is Lulan Li. I major in molecular evolution, in botany. It is my honor to have this opportunity to exchange and discuss with all of the professional researchers. And I am glad to share some of my study with you.

Firstly, I want to ask you a question: As for the nine kinds of supernatural Chinese medicinal herbs, can you tell me their names? Ginseng, Ganoderma, snow lotus, anything else? Which one is the first of them?

It is Dendrobium officinale.

Now I am here to talk to you about a precious herb—Dendrobium officinale (Orchidaceae), which is ranked "the first of the nine kinds of supernatural Chinese medicinal herbs". Dendrobium officinale, as a tonic herb in Chinese materia medica and health food in folk, has been utilized for the treatment of yin-deficiency diseases for decades.

So in this presentation, I focus on the medicinal value and application research of Dendrobium officinale.

I have divided my presentation into three parts: (a) the habitat of Dendrobium officinale; (b) the functions of Dendrobium officinale; (c) the industrialization of Dendrobium officinale.

If you have any questions, I will be glad to answer them after the presentation.

1. _____
2. _____

3. _____

4. _____
5. _____

6. _____

7. _____

8. _____

1.7 Suppose now you are giving a speech on the impact of the Internet on society. Prepare with your partner for an effective introduction by using attention grabbers to lead in your topic or thesis statement. The following items should be included to help you organize your introduction in logic and you can use the useful expressions in the box.

- Greeting the audience;
- Introducing yourself;
- Using attention grabbers;
- Unveiling the topic;
- Stating the thesis statement;
- Previewing the main points;
- Predicting the Q & A plan.

 Useful Expressions

How to Start Your Speech

- Good morning, ladies and gentlemen, let me introduce myself…
- I am honored/privileged/pleased to have this opportunity of presenting my study on…
- Today I am going to talk about… / This morning I'd like to present… / The purpose of my presentation is to overview… / What I want to do is to illustrate…
- I have broken/divided my speech into…parts. / I will concentrate on the following points:…
- If you have any questions, I'll be happy to answer them as we go along. / Feel free to ask any questions. / Do feel free to interrupt me if you have any questions.

1.8 Now deliver the introduction you have prepared in front of the class and other students may comment on the attention grabbers you have used.

Students	Attention Grabbers	Comments on the Attention Grabbers
1		

(Continued)

Students	Attention Grabbers	Comments on the Attention Grabbers
2		
3		
4		
5		

Section 2

Ending a Speech

2.1 Read the following closing speech by Steve Jobs on the Commencement of Stanford University on June 12, 2005. Then fulfill the tasks.

When I was young, there was an amazing publication called *The Whole Earth Catalog*, which was one of the bibles of my generation. It was created by a fellow named Stewart Brand, not far from here in Menlo Park, and he brought it to life with his poetic touch. This was in the late 1960s, before personal computers and desktop publishing, so it was all made with typewriters, scissors, and Polaroid cameras. It was sort of like Google in paperback form, 35 years before Google came along: It was idealistic, and overflowing with neat tools and great notion.

Stewart and his team put out several issues of *The Whole Earth Catalog*, and then when it had run its course, they put out a final issue. It was the mid 1970s, and I was your age. On the back cover of their final issue was a photograph of an early morning country road, the kind you might find yourself hitchhiking on if you were so adventurous. Beneath it were the words: "Stay Hungry. Stay Foolish." It was their farewell message as they signed off.

Stay Hungry. Stay Foolish. And I have always wished that for myself. And now, as you graduate to begin anew, I wish that for you.

Stay Hungry. Stay Foolish.

Thank you all very much.

1. Discuss with your partner and make some comments on how the speech comes to an end.

2. Work with your partner to complete the sentences below.

(1) The speech ends with the anecdote about the final issue of an amazing publication *The Whole Earth Catalog* in the mid-1970s, because _____

_____

_____ .

(2) From your perspective, "Stay Hungry. Stay Foolish." means _____

_____

_____ .

(3) After sharing the anecdote, Steve Jobs expresses _____ to the audience.

2.2 Read the following speech endings. Then fulfill the tasks.

1. Compare normal endings with those with a bang. What strategies are used to make the latter impressive?

Normal Endings	Endings with a Bang
a. That's the end of my presentation. Thank you for your attention.	a. We've had a great discussion today about what software will look like in the near future; I'd like to close by asking you what you think software might look like 100 years from now. Are we actually heading for the Great Singularity? Thank you.
b. So much for my presentation. Thank you.	
c. That concludes my presentation. Thank you for your listening.	b. Before I finish my speech, I'd like to share with you a short message from Michael Jordan who is a sponsor for the Iowa Life Gift Coalition on Organ and Tissue Donor Awareness, which appears in their 1996 brochure: "Please make the decision to become an organ and tissue donor. Remember: Share your life. Share your decision." Thank you, ladies and gentlemen. （陈美华，2013）
d. That's all. Thank you very much.	

(Continued)

Normal Endings	Endings with a Bang
	c. And so, my message to you is this: We need to use these tools. We need to secure our telephone calls. We need to secure our text messages. I want you to use these tools. I want you to tell your loved ones. I want you to tell your colleagues: Use these encrypted communication tools. Don't just use them because they're cheap and easy, but use them because they're secure. Thank you. (Adapted from the TED Talk "How to Avoid Surveillance… with the Phone in Your Pocket".)

2. Discuss with your partner and describe the strategies used in the right column and what effect the speakers want to achieve by using them.

(1) The first speaker ends the speech with _____, which can
_____.

(2) The second speaker ends the speech with _____, which can
_____.

(3) The third speaker ends the speech with _____, which can
_____.

2.3 Read the paper "Musical Training Can Accelerate Brain Development and Help with Literacy Skills". Then fulfill the tasks.

1. Make a conclusion of the research in the paper. The following items should be included to help you organize your conclusion in logic and you can use the useful expressions in the box.

   - Summarizing the main points;
   - Presenting an ending with certain strategies;
   - Thanking the audience;
   - Inviting questions.

 Useful Expressions

How to Close Your Speech

(1) Making a Summary:
   - At this stage, I would like to run through/over the main points.
   - Finally, I'd like to remind you of some of the main points we've considered.
   - So, as we have seen today... ·

(2) Presenting an Ending:
   - I would like to end the presentation by quoting...
   - As a result, we suggest that...

(3) Inviting Questions:
   - Now I'd like to answer your questions, if you have any.
   - Now I am ready to answer your questions.
   - Please don't hesitate to ask me if you have any questions.

2. Then present your conclusion in front of the class. Other students may make some comments on the strategies you have used to conclude.

Students	Comments on Strategies
1	
2	
3	
4	

3
Chapter

Arguing Sufficiently

Warm-up Questions:

1. What will you say to make your statement "People are facing serious environment problems every day" convincing enough?

2. What can you do to help the audience understand your presentation better?

To establish our points of view effectively, we need to develop it with enough evidence. Therefore, the body of a presentation develops the thesis statement with several main points, each of which is well-supported by evidence or details. Besides, the evidence is laid out in certain logic. The swarming information might make it difficult for the audience to follow the speaker. Then the use of signposts is quite necessary to guide the audience from one point to another.

Section 1 Main Points

1.1 Read the article "Global Warming and Its Effects". Then make a list of the main points which you think are important for understanding the article.

_____

_____

_____

_____

_____

1.2 In groups, present some of the main points listed above in three minutes. Remember to select the facts and statistics that are the most significant or relevant to support the main points. The following is an example.

Main Point	Facts and Statistics
The effects of global warming	• Increase of floods and droughts; • Disappearance of 95% of the Great Barrier Reef by 2075; • Melting of Glacier National Park by 2030; • Extinction of 37% of all species by 2050.

1.3 **While one student gives his or her presentation, the others in each group should complete the following assessment form and write down their suggestions for improvement.**

Assessments	Yes or No?
There is an overview of the topic and main points at the beginning.	
Each main point is sufficiently supported.	
The presenter moves from one point to another clearly.	
The presenter adds his or her own views to the main points.	
The visual aids are used effectively.	
The presenter pauses appropriately to attract the audience's attention.	
The presenter summarizes the main points at the end.	

Suggestions:

_____

_____

_____

1.4 **Read the following paragraphs and make comments on the relation between the main point and the supporting evidence in each paragraph.**

1. And increasingly, over the last couple of years, Silicon Valley companies have built strong encryption technology into their communication products that makes surveillance extremely difficult. For example, many of you have an iPhone, and if you use an iPhone to send a text message to other people who have an iPhone, those text messages can't be wiretapped easily. (Adapted from the TED Talk "Safeguard Your Privacy".)

> The speaker hopes to illustrate the effect of encryption technology with _____
> _____.

2. Since 1901, medicine has advanced greatly. We've discovered antibiotics and vaccines to protect us from infections, many treatments for cancer, antiretrovirals for HIV, statins for heart disease, and much more. But we've made essentially no progress at all in treating Alzheimer's disease. (Adapted from the TED Talk "Alzheimer's Is Not Normal Aging—And We Can Cure It".)

> The speaker develops his speech by _____ great advance in treating infections, cancers, HIV, and heart disease with no progress in treating Alzheimer's disease.

3. We understand less about the science of Alzheimer's than other diseases because we've invested less time and money into researching it. The U.S. government spends 10 times more every year on cancer research than on Alzheimer's despite the fact that Alzheimer's costs us more and causes a similar number of deaths each year as cancer. The lack of resources stems from a more fundamental cause: a lack of awareness. Because here's what few people know but everyone should know: Alzheimer's is a disease, and we can cure it. (ibid.)

> The speaker analyzes the _____ for the fact that we know less about Alzheimer's disease.

4. First, what are the causes of sleep deprivation? Why don't we get enough sleep? You may be surprised to learn that our modern lifestyle—that's, the way we live our life—creates many of our sleep problems. People today are very busy; they're working more and more hours every day. In fact, did you know that more than 30% of American adults work more than fifty hours a week? Well, as a result, there's less time to do other things, like reading or paying bills or cleaning house, so people stay up later and get less sleep. （蔡基刚，2012）

> The speaker investigates into the _____ of our inability to fall asleep at night.

5. So, most people feel sleepy during the day. One consequence of this is making mistakes at work. Without enough sleep, we don't function well—we don't have enough energy and…eh…we can't always think very clearly. And there are many people at work each day who need more sleep. About 50% of Americans say they're usually sleepy at work. And about 20% say they make mistakes at work because they're sleepy. These mistakes can cost a lot of money or cause accidents that hurt or even kill people. (ibid.)

> The speaker displays the _____ of lacking enough sleep during the day.

Section 2

Logic Patterns

2.1 Think about the following logic patterns that might be used to develop a speech.

Logic Patterns:
- Chronological/sequential order;
- Description/enumeration pattern;
- Comparison and contrast pattern;
- Cause and effect pattern;
- Problem-solution pattern.

2.2 You are supposed to prepare for a presentation on global warming. Discuss with your partner about which logic pattern you will choose to give the following presentations. Exchange your reasons.

Presentation Topics:
- The Present Situation of Global Warming
- The Global Temperature Rise
- Global Warming in 1930s and That in 2000
- A Low Carbon Life
- Population Booming and Economic Development

2.3 Now prepare for an outline of your presentation on global warming in different logic patterns. In groups, choose one of the logic patterns below. Work together to form one main point of global warming and collect some evidence to support it.

Logic Pattern 1	Chronological order
Main Point	
Supporting Evidence	

Logic Pattern 2	Enumeration pattern
Main Point	
Supporting Evidence	

Logic Pattern 3	Comparison and contrast pattern
Main Point	
Supporting Evidence	

Logic Pattern 4	Cause and effect pattern
Main Point	
Supporting Evidence	

Logic Pattern 5	Problem-solution pattern
Main Point	
Supporting Evidence	

2.4 Present your outline in front of the class. Other students may write down what logic pattern the presentation follows.

Presenters	Logic Patterns
1	
2	
3	
4	
5	

Section 3   Signposts

Signposts help listeners follow your messages in an oral presentation. As signposts are used on the road to show you how far your exit is, signposts in a presentation are used to engage the audience and bring them through different stages.

3.1 **In groups, one student reads the article "Causes and Effects of Sleep Deprivation" loud to the group and the other members answer the following questions while listening. They may ask him or her to pause whenever they think he or she is hitting the point, so that they can win some time to write down the answers.**

1. What is the problem the speaker is talking about?

_____

_____

2. Why does the presentation begin with some questions?

_____

_____

3. What is the thesis statement of the presentation? Where is it?

_____

_____

4. The information from the survey conducted by the National Sleep Center is developed in a cause and effect pattern. What words or expressions guide your attention to causes and effects respectively?

(1) Indicators for causes: _____

_____

Cause 1: _____

Cause 2: _____

(2) Indicators for effects: _____

_____

Effect 1: _____

Effect 2: _____

3.2 **Read the article above to see whether you have followed your group member through his or her reading. Think about what helps you maintain your attention to the key points.**

1. What are the transitional words showing that the speaker is moving from one point to another?

_____

_____

2.   What questions are used in the body of the presentation? What is the purpose?

_____

_____

3.   Why does the speaker repeat the sentence "So most people feel sleepy during the day"?

_____

_____

4.   What is the function of "so" in the presentation?

_____

_____

5.   What linguistic means are used to signpost the development of the presentation?

_____

_____

What Is a Signpost?

A signpost is defined as a device which writers or speakers use to let their readers or listeners know which direction their writing or speech is moving. Signposts are very important in writing and speeches as they help people to follow what you are writing or saying. Different types of transitions, rhetoric questions, repeated use of words and sentence patterns, as well as intonation and stress, can act as signposts.

3.3 Read the following useful expressions and think about how you will use them to develop your presentation.

(1)   Expressions to Introduce a Point:

- First of all / To begin with / In the first place...
- I'd like to start by...
- Let's begin with...
- Now let us look at the first aspect which is...

(2)   Expressions to Shift Among Points (or Topics):

- Well, let's move on to the next point.
- So much for / That's all for...and now we can go on to / turn to...
- Now that we have seen...and let us examine it more closely.
- We have talked here about...Now I'd like to explain...

(3) Expressions to Elaborate on a Point:

- I suppose this part is the most difficult, so let's discuss it at length. / I'd like to go into detail. / I shall talk about it in detail.
- I'd like to deal with the third part of my presentation more extensively.
- As to the last point of my presentation, I'd like to spend more minutes on it.

(4) Expressions to Underline Important Points:

- This is important because…
- Please notice that…
- What is very important is…
- I'd like to emphasize the fact that…

(5) Expressions to Analyze a Point:

- Where does that lead us?
- Let's consider this in more detail.
- What does this mean for…?
- What exactly are the benefits?

(6) Expressions to Summarize Main Points:

- Summarizing what we just talked about…
- To summarize…
- In summary, this report found…

3.4 Read the following descriptions of the bad effects of smartphones. In groups, work out the main point described and the relevant supporting evidence in each paragraph.

Bad Effects of Smartphones

Smartphones may let you surf the Internet, listen to music, and snap photos wherever you are. But it seems that they also turn you into a workaholic. A study suggests that, by giving you access to e-mails at all times, the all-singing, all-dancing mobile phone adds as much as two hours to your working day. Researchers found that Britons work an additional 460 hours a year on average as they are able to respond to e-mails on their mobiles.

A new research has revealed that using a computer or smartphone at night can cause us to pile on the pounds. The study found a link between blue light exposure—blue light is emitted by smartphones and tablets—and increased hunger. It found that exposure to the light increases hunger levels for several hours and even increases hunger levels after you eat a meal. Blue light exposure has also been shown to decreased sleepiness in the evening, increasing the risk of insomnia.

The number of mobile phone users has grown—to about 77% of the world's population, the study says—so has the number of phone-related accidents. The number of the U.S. emergency-room visits linked to phone use on the move doubled to as many as 1,500 between 2005 and 2010, recently showed by an Ohio State University study.

As well as distracting students from their studies, experts say it is damaging interpersonal skills. "Students today are very bad at reading facial expressions," said Setsuko Tamura, a professor of applied psychology at Tokyo Seitoku University, "When you spend more time texting people instead of talking to them, you don't learn how to read non-verbal language."

1.   **Paragraph 1:**

Main Point: _____

Supporting Evidence: _____

_____

_____

_____

2.   **Paragraph 2:**

Main Point: _____

Supporting Evidence: _____

_____

_____

_____

3.   **Paragraph 3 :**

Main Point: _____

Supporting Evidence: _____

_____

_____

_____

4.   **Paragraph 4 :**

Main Point: _____

Supporting Evidence: _____

_____

_____

_____

3.5 In groups, make a presentation for each main point and its supporting evidence in 3.4 by using the expressions in 3.3.

3.6 Discuss with your partner about the effects of a presentation by using signposts.

4 Chapter

Delivering a Presentation

Warm-up Questions:

1. In what ways is an oral presentation different from a scientific paper?

2. What do you think is a successful presentation?

3. What can you do to make a successful presentation?

4. Will you consider your audience when you give a presentation?

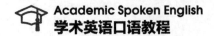
How can we enhance the impact of our presentation? Visual aids are what the audience can see. PPTs, posters, handouts, as well as texts and graphics appeal directly to the audience. The effective use of body language also adds power to our speech since we communicate our attitudes, intentions, and feelings to the audience through different non-verbal languages. Even our voice may contribute to a good presentation. Pausing, slowing down, and raising or lowering the voice definitely enable the audience to follow our presentation.

Section 1   **Presentation Skills**

1.1 What are you worried about in delivering a good presentation? Discuss with your partner and add more to the list.

I'm worried about:

- Language skills in the presentation;
- Professional limits in my research;
- Being nervous during the presentation;
- Reaction from the audience;
- Questions from the audience.

_____

_____

_____

_____

_____

_____

_____

_____

1.2 PPT is commonly used in presentations. The following statements introduce the design and the use of PPT.

1. In groups, discuss and decide whether they are effective or not.

Design and Use of PPT	Effective or Not?
I put a whole paragraph from my paper on the slide so that the audience can know more about my research.	
A colorful slide is more attractive.	
PPT is convenient so that I can read the text on the slide.	
To highlight my points, I put all the text in the bold type.	
Since the information is on the slide, I might leave it for the audience to read on their own.	
I prefer to use complete sentences rather than words and expressions on the slide.	
I show the audience the graphics one by one without saying anything.	

2. If the statements above are not effective enough, how can we design or use PPT in a correct way? Make a discussion in groups. Then make a summary of the ideas in front of the class.

1.3 Look at the two slides below. The first is used to lead in the topic of the speech and the second is an overview of the main points. Present the beginning of a presentation by using the two slides below. You can also follow the useful expressions in the box.

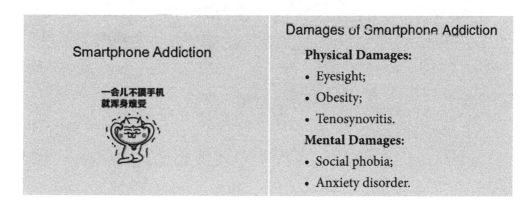

How to Turn to Visual Aids

- Take a look at this… / Let's have a look at this. / I'd like you to look at this. / Here we can see… / I'd like to draw your attention to…
- The…represents…and the…shows…
- OK, so you can see a summary of our results here…
- On this graph, … / The graph illustrates…
- From the information given, it can be concluded/inferred/assumed that…
- The information given in the graph implies/suggests/hints that…

1.4 Work with your partner to describe the chart and the table below.

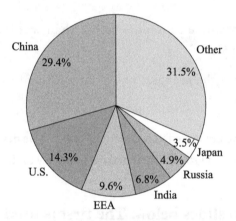

Figure 4-1　Global carbon dioxide emissions by country in 2015

Table 4-1　The average scores achieved by boys and girls of different ages in several subjects in local schools

Age of Boys	Subjects				
	Math	History	Geography	English	P. E.
7	63	70	63	62	71
10	65	72	68	60	74
13	69	74	70	60	75
15	67	73	64	58	78

(Continued)

Age of Girls	Subjects				
	Math	History	Geography	English	P. E.
7	64	69	62	62	65
10	65	73	64	67	64
13	64	70	62	65	62
15	68	72	64	75	60

Tips

How to Use Visual Aids Effectively

- Keep the visuals simple and clear.
- Speak to the audience rather than visuals.
- Use the right font size (titles: 38–44 points; text: 28–32 points).
- Use contrasting colors.
- Expand and explain visual information.
- Avoid language errors.

1.5 Work in groups. You read the following excerpt from the article "Birds Learn Each Other's "Languages" by Listening, Experts Say". Then fulfill the tasks.

Christopher Templeton is a biologist at Pacific University in Forest Grove, Oregon, who was not involved in the study. "Until this study, we had limited knowledge about how an animal learns what calls from other species actually mean," Templeton said. "What this new study does is removing the predator entirely. It shows that these birds can learn to associate new sounds with danger, without having to learn them through trial and error," he added.

Andrew Radford of the University of Bristol noted that the ability to learn to link sounds with meaning makes biological sense. "If you can only learn in the presence of a predator, that's quite dangerous," he said.

1. Ask your partner to mark where you control your breath while listening.

2. Listen to the excerpt above and notice where the announcer pauses to take a breath. Compare whether you pause at the same place.

Sense Groups

With the limited span of memory, it is not easy for listeners to remember longer stretches of information. Therefore, to keep the communication effective, speakers would utter a few words at a time. This brief unit of word series is called a sense group, which is identified by pause before or after it. Relative pronouns, conjunctions, and prepositions are common grammatical words to introduce a sense group.

1.6 Watch the TED Talk "Your Fingerprints Reveal More Than You Think". Then answer the following questions.

1. Does the speaker speak fast or slowly? Do you prefer to deliver a presentation at a fast pace or at a slow pace? Give your reasons.

   _____

   _____

   _____

2. Why does she speak word by word at the beginning? Why does she speak fast with the sentence "I've just left my fingerprints all over my wine glass"?

   _____

   _____

   _____

3. Why does she pause a little when she finishes raising the questions: "Or do you ever worry, when you visit a friend, about leaving a little piece of you behind on every surface that you touch? And even this evening, have you paid any attention to sit without touching anything?"

   _____

   _____

   _____

4. Where does the speaker raise her voice? Where does she lower her voice? What is the purpose?

   _____

   _____

   _____

5. How does the speaker speak in a rhythmic way? Where does she pause a little? Where does she speed up?

_____

_____

_____

6. What does the speaker do to emphasize some ideas or facts?

_____

_____

_____

7. Does the speaker use any body language? What is it? Where does she do so?

_____

_____

_____

8. Does the speaker use any visual aids? Why does she use them?

_____

_____

_____

1.7 Work with your partner and discuss how to deliver a presentation.

1. Judge whether the following performances are good or bad in an academic presentation.

Performances	Good or Bad?
Say hello and smile when you greet the audience.	
Use a lot of slides.	
Put information as much as possible in each slide.	
Walk around a little and gesture with your hands.	
Look at the screen while speaking, and move on to the audience once in a while.	
Read the notes.	
Look at someone in the audience while speaking.	

2. Think over whether there are some other performances that should be avoided.

Other Performances:

_____

_____

_____

1.8 You are supposed to give a presentation on global warming in five minutes. Other students should evaluate your presentation in terms of the following items in the form.

1. Ask students to evaluate your presentation by "Good (G)", "Just so so (S)", or "Bad (B)" in each item.

Students	Pronunciation	Intonation	Volume	Speed	Eye Contact	Visual Aids
1						
2						
3						
4						
5						
6						

2. After that, you can summarize the failures in your presentation together with your partner. Think about whether there are any other factors that may damage your presentation.

Other Factors:

_____

_____

_____

Poster Display

Both oral presentations and poster presentations are popular in academic conferences. Besides abstracts and papers, academic conferences may also call for posters. Participants can attend poster sessions to present their research.

2.1 Read the "Call for Posters" from an international conference below. Then discuss the following questions with your partner.

The International Conference on Innovations in Business, Economics, Management, Social Sciences conference poster session will provide an opportunity for authors to interact informally with conference attendees, using a standard-size poster as a visual aid. Presenting a poster is also a good way to discuss and receive feedback on a work in progress that has not been fully developed into a paper. To facilitate this interaction, the conference poster session will be held in conference common areas, where attention of the participants is expected to be high.

1.   Where will the poster session be held? Why?

_____

_____

2.   What is the special requirement on posters?

_____

_____

3. How can authors interact informally with conference attendees in poster sessions?

_____

_____

4. According to the conference notice, what are the advantages of poster sessions? What do you think of these advantages?

_____

_____

_____

_____

2.2 Search for some academic posters on the Internet. Then discuss the following questions with your partner.

1. What information can you find in the poster? Is it similar to that in an oral presentation?

_____

_____

_____

_____

2. What do you prefer to perform in an international academic conference, an oral presentation or a poster presentation? Give your reasons.

_____

_____

_____

_____

3. What is an effective poster in your opinion? The following are some of the problems that make posters ineffective, including: (a) objective(s) and main point(s) hard to find; (b) too small text size; (c) poor graphics; (d) poor organization. Work with your partner to think about more problems so that you can avoid them in making effective posters.

_____

_____

_____

_____

2.3 Work with your partner at the poster below and answer the questions.

The Physical and Mental Damage from Smartphone

Name, Affiliation

Email, Address

Introduction
Mobile phone are becoming commonplace in college classrooms. The hush-hush chitchat between back-benchers is gradually being replaced by whispered phone conversations and SMSchats. Hip and convenient, they are used for everything from playing games to planning a sudden outing.

Most teachers and students agree that cell phones interfere with the teaching process. Professors find it difficult to command attention and encourage participation if students receive calls during class. It upsets the rhythm of the class.

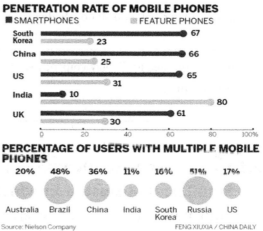

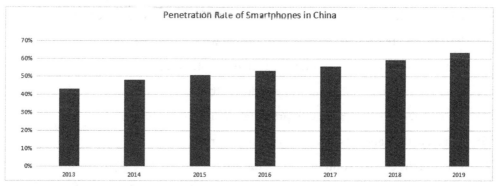

Results
• 70% of the subjects suffer from near-sightedness and presbyopia before 40 years old
• 63% are overweighted
• 90% have sore thumbs
• 93% would rather stay alone with their smartphones
• 56% need to use drugs to control their anxiety

Conclusion
Physical damages:
• eyesight
• obesity
• tenosynovitis
Mental damages:
• social phobia
• anxiety disorder

1. What information of the paper may be available on the top of the poster?

_____

2. Imagine you are a visitor looking over this poster, what aspect of the research do you want to discuss with the researcher?

_____

3. Which is more friendly to you, the static poster contents or the fluent oral presentation? Why?

_____

4. At some conferences, researchers are not necessarily in the poster area. If you are the poster owner, will you stand beside it all the time? Why or why not?

_____

5. Is it a good idea to display your poster in your tablet instead of on a board? Discuss with your partner.

_____

2.4 Suppose you are attending a poster session on global warming. Simulate that session in which you are a poster presenter and your partner is a questioner.

1. Discuss with your partner what you will do to keep the session in effect.

(1) If someone approaches you and your poster, what should you do?

(2) What does the questioner want to say to the poster presenter?

(3) If no one has come yet, what will you do to attract the passers-by?

(4) Do you need to prepare an oral presentation in a poster session?

(5) What are the handouts of your poster used for?

2. Perform the conversation in front of the class.

3. The questioner then makes some comments on the poster design and the poster display in terms of the following evaluations.

Evaluations	Yes or No?
The poster is made up of different sections from introduction to conclusion.	
The contents are eligible two meters away.	
When introducing the poster, the speaker reads from notes.	

(Continued)

Evaluations	Yes or No?
The speaker greets me warmly.	
The speaker turns his or her back to me from time to time.	
The speaker moves his or her gaze between the poster and me.	
The colors are carefully chosen to highlight important information.	
The speaker professionally answers my questions.	
The speaker keeps silent while I am viewing the poster.	
The title and the speaker's information are prominent and eye-catching.	

Tips

How to Perform Well in a Poster Session

- Stand closer to your poster.
- Wear your name tag.
- Smile and make eye contact.
- Greet viewers actively.
- Leave time for viewers to read your poster.
- Don't get involved with one person.
- Prepare handouts.

2.5 In groups, discuss the differences between poster display and oral presentation.

1.　Talk about their advantages and disadvantages in terms of the items on the left of the form below.

Items	Poster Display	Oral Presentation
Time		
Numbers of presenters		

(Continued)

Items	Poster Display	Oral Presentation
Numbers of questions		
Atmosphere		
Interaction		
Methods to introduce		
Cost		

2. Decide in your group which has more advantages. Give your reasons.

2.6 Put the contents of your presentation on global warming in Section 2, Chapter 3 into a poster. Display the poster to your partner and perform it in front of the class.

 Extensive Reading

Although viewed by some people in the scientific community as inferior to other forms of communication in the greater science and engineering community, the poster is an extremely powerful form of communication at professional conferences. Advantages of poster sessions over oral presentations include the length of the time allotted for discussion at professional meetings. Most oral presentations are limited to about 15 minutes unless they are invited plenary. Poster sessions on the other hand often allow for two hours or more of discussion with interested visitors. In addition, at most meetings multiple oral presentations are scheduled to run simultaneously in small rooms allowing for a very limited number of audience. Poster sessions often take place in large rooms and accommodate hundreds of presenters. Consequently, there is greater potential exposure of your work to the greater scientific community in poster sessions.

5
Chapter

Practicing Your Presentation

We give oral presentations in many situations, from dinner toast, classroom presentations, thesis defense, to job interview, plan design, etc. Among them, classroom presentations are now popular in teaching, with the purpose to enhance the learning and evaluate the teaching effect. Students show their understanding of a certain topic in classroom presentations. Thesis defense presentations, however, require students to defend their original research effectively and prove their qualification for degrees. After graduation, students will attend job interview presentations to impress the interview panels and win a desirable post.

Section 1 / Classroom Presentations

1.1 Make a survey about popular Internet words or expressions with your partner.

1. Make a list of some popular Internet words or expressions and work out their origins and meanings.

   _____

   _____

   _____

2. Answer the questions below.

(1) Why are the words or expressions so popular among young people? Give at least two reasons.

   _____

   _____

   _____

(2) Do you think it is appropriate for students to use these words or expressions in their compositions or papers? Give your reasons.

   _____

   _____

   _____

3. Present the results of your survey to the class. Remember to state your purpose of the presentation, express the main points, and draw a conclusion finally.

1.2 Do you often shop online? Exchange your answers in pairs.

1.   What do you usually buy on the Internet?

_____

_____

2.   What is the most satisfying or dissatisfying product you have bought?

_____

_____

1.3 Read the article "The Continued Appeal of Online Shopping". Then answer the following questions.

1.   Why is shopping online thriving according to the article? Find as many reasons as you can. Do not repeat the sentences in the article. Try to use your own words.

Reason 1: _____

Reason 2: _____

Reason 3: _____

Reason 4: _____

Reason 5: _____

Reason 6: _____

Reason 7: _____

2.   Which do you prefer, shopping online or going to a real shop? Give your reasons.

_____

_____

_____

_____

1.3 Present your opinions on online shopping to the class. Remember to give a brief introduction before the main points and make a conclusion after the main points.

1.4 Watch the video clip of *The Big Bang Theory* (Episode 3, Season 2). Then answer the following questions.

1. What reasons are given in the video clip for Penny's addiction to computer games?

   _____

   _____

   _____

2. Do you have more reasons for Internet or game addiction?

   _____

   _____

   _____

1.5 Read the article "Internet Addiction: The New Mental Health Disorder?". Then identify the main points in the article.

Symptoms of Internet Addiction:

_____

_____

_____

_____

Effects of Internet Addiction:

_____

_____

_____

_____

Treatments:

_____

_____

_____

_____

1.6 Brainstorm the positive and negative impacts of the Internet on our life.

Positive Impacts:

_____

_____

_____

_____

Negative Impacts:

_____

_____

_____

_____

1.7 You are supposed to prepare and give a presentation about the impact of Internet on our life in five minutes by using PPT. While listening to your presentation, the other students may complete the following evaluation form. Put a "√" in the appropriate box (1=bad; 2=just so so; 3=good).

Evaluations	1	2	3
A clear and complete thesis statement.			
Clear main points.			
Enough eye contact.			
Different body languages for different purposes.			
Speed, pitch, and tone are varied for certain effects.			
Use of visual aids to make the presentation more clear and interesting.			
Well organized by introduction, body, and ending.			
Effective use of signposts to indicate the development of the presentation.			
An appealing beginning.			
A perfect summary.			

Tips

The Simple Structure of Speeches

- Tell the audience what you're going to tell them.
- Tell them.
- Tell them what you have told them.

Job Interview Presentations

Job interview presentations are becoming more and more common, especially for more senior level roles. Presentations give employers the opportunity to see how candidates perform in the less structured way than they do in a traditional interview.

2.1 Work with your partner to answer the following questions.

1. Have you given any job interview presentations? If yes, please describe your experience (e.g. when and where, topic, purpose, main contents, etc.).

   _____

   _____

   _____

2. What abilities can be shown in your job interview presentation?

   _____

   _____

   _____

3. What do you think is the key to a successful job interview presentation?

   _____

   _____

   _____

2.2 Sarah posted a question on the website and then she got some helpful answers.

1. Look at Sarah's post below. What is her problem?

> I've just been told that I have a job interview next Wednesday. I need to do a 10-minute presentation in front of the other candidates followed by a formal interview. The topic of the presentation is "What I can bring to this position" and "How I will adapt to make my job successful". I've never had to do anything like this before and I just don't know where to start!

2. Two answers on the website are listed below. Read them and work with your partner to figure out the useful suggestions.

> **Answer from Stefan:** I am also preparing for an interview myself. I have to present myself and let them know what I will bring to the team. I have started my report by saying who I am, my academic background and now I am thinking of talking about my business qualifications and how my present job experience helps me be more responsible, organized, and a better problem-solver. I will present some cases where I was highly involved and that will show my professional attitude and mentality.
>
> **Answer from Rach:** I have been offered the following advice for my 10-minute presentation for an interview this coming Tuesday, so I'm sharing it with you. I will be given the topic and given an hour to prepare it.
>
> *   The structure contains three parts: (a) tell them what you are going to tell them; (b) tell them; (c) tell them what you told them.
> *   You should use minimal flip charts or slides, no more than four. I would aim at three if possible.
> *   Start with an introduction "I am", "I will be talking about…", and "I will allow time for questions (at the end)".
> *   Depending upon what subject you get, you may wish to consider using the SWOT analysis method of delivery which should contain about three or four strengths, weaknesses, opportunities, and threats. I often find subjects or the questions asked don't fit easily into SWOT and should that be the case it is perhaps best to use the rule of three.
> *   Pick what your focal point will be (i.e. Our company should wear green ties not red ties).
> *   Presuming that you will be given a flip chart at least, I would divide the body of the presentation into three points, and use a separate flip chart for each point. For example, discussing the cost, availability, and quality.

> • Conclude with a summary backing up your point and maybe even a catch phrase or saying.
>
> There are other notes of advice: Adhere strictly to time, and try not to over complicate it. Don't talk to the flip chart, and practice it if you have time. In terms of preparation before the day, rack your brains for questions and practice it at home. This will mean that your introduction will essentially be the same and a little bit like a "fill in the blanks".

Suggestions:

_____

_____

_____

2.3 Suppose you are attending a job interview for teaching in your school. You are required to make a presentation on Sarah's topic mentioned in 2.2 in five minutes. Then answer the following questions.

1.　What do you want to say at the beginning of your presentation?

_____

_____

_____

2.　What about the body part of your presentation?

_____

_____

_____

3.　How will you finish the presentation?

_____

_____

_____

2.4 In groups, one student delivers the presentation while the other students, acting as the interview panel, evaluate it. Put a "√" in the appropriate box (1=bad; 2=just so so; 3=good).

Evaluations	1	2	3
The applicant behaves confidently by making appropriate eye contact with the panel.			
At the beginning of the presentation, the applicant introduces the topic, the outline, and the subsequent main points.			
The applicant highlights his or her advantages for the position by stressing the key words from time to time to avoid being monotonous.			
The applicant keeps smiling while delivering the presentation.			
PPTs make the presentation clearer.			
The applicant slows down at the important qualifications.			
The applicant speaks fluently, which indicates a good preparation.			
Finally, the applicant summarizes his or her advantages over other applicants.			

Section 3

Thesis Defense Presentations

The thesis defense is an oral presentation and examination after finishing the writing process of thesis. The student has to answer the questions from the thesis defense committee members. To perform well in this session, he or she had better expect questions beforehand.

3.1 Discuss the following questions with your partner.

1.　Does your school hold an "open" or "closed" thesis defense?

2.　How many committee members are required? Who would be the chairperson?

3.　How long should your presentation last?

4.　What preparations are necessary for a successful thesis defense?

3.2 Read the article "Presentation of Thesis Defense". Then work together with your partner and complete the following sentences.

1.　The purpose of the first three paragraphs is to _____
_____
_____ .

2.　Paragraphs 4 and 5 introduce _____
_____
_____ .

3.　Paragraphs 6–11 lay out _____
_____
_____ .

4.　Paragraph 12 shows _____
_____
_____ .

5.　Paragraphs 13–15 introduce _____
_____
_____ .

6.　Paragraph 16 summarizes _____
_____
_____ .

3.3 Read the following questions that we need to prepare for our thesis defense presentation. Then think about whether the presentation in 3.2 has covered the questions. If yes, write down the paragraph number(s) of each question.

Questions	Paragraph Numbers
What is the focus of your research?	
What have you argued?	
What important points have you demonstrated in your thesis?	
What is your methodology?	
What is your contribution to the relevant field?	
What are the weaker points of your thesis?	

3.4 Read the Discussion section of a paper. Suppose it is your research. Then in your thesis defense, what would you like to say about the first two questions in 3.3? Make a presentation in front of the class.

 Extensive Reading

Job Interview Presentations

Passage 1: If you have succeeded in getting to the final interview for a professional job in higher education, the chance is that you will be asked to deliver a short presentation to the panel. You will usually be given a specific topic to prepare: Typically this might be to address a current issue and make recommendations on how you would tackle this issue in post. For teaching positions, you may be asked to deliver a lesson to an invited audience or to the panel.

The panel are usually judging:
- The quality of your ideas;
- The clarity of your thinking—for example, if you are able to take a strategic perspective;
- Your verbal communication skills, especially your ability to influence and engage your audience;

- Your organization skills: How well you prepare beforehand and manage your time within the presentation;
- Your formal presentation skills which are a key part of the job.

Passage 2: If you have a job interview that includes a presentation, in general, restrict your presentation to three main sections. This helps to keep a strong focus on your speech. Three tends to be the magic number that people remember things in and it is easier to follow and make the audience remember the message and you as a speaker. Your presentation should follow the following structure:

- Section 1: Beginning
  - The aim—what is the message that you want to convey?
  - What the presentation contains—tell the audience what you're going to say.
- Section 2: Middle
  - Deliver—tell them.
- Section 3: End
  - Recap and summarize—tell them what you've told them.

Your presentation must convey one key message which will act like a backbone for the presentation and should hold everything else together. It is important that you make a strong opening at the start of the presentation. This is the time when you want to grab the interviewers' attention. There are a few ways of doing this. For instance, you might start with a question, or a quote, or an important fact to arouse interest. A good start will set the tone for the rest of your presentation.

6 Chapter

Seminars

1. What is a seminar? Have you attended any seminars?

2. Are you brave enough to state your viewpoints in a seminar? If yes, what builds up your confidence? If not, what is the problem?

3. What are the responsibilities of the leader in a seminar?

Among the international students, Chinese students are criticized most often for their least intention to attend the class discussion actively. They would rather sit in the classroom and listen passively in quietness. A professor complains: "No matter how hard I encourage Chinese students, they refuse to speak their minds." In fact, to effectively communicate our academic ideas and research, it is essential to attend seminars. Therefore, some basic knowledge about seminars might help us conquer our uneasiness in communication. Meanwhile, the ability to understand others is also conducive to building our confidence in seminars.

Section 1 / Attending a Seminar

1.1 **Watch the video clip of *The Big Bang Theory* (Episode 13, Season 4) and try to describe to your partner what a seminar is like. The words in the box are helpful to your description.**

participants	seminar leader	particular subject	opinions	seminar room

_____

_____

_____

_____

1.2 **Read the definition of "seminar" below. Then answer the following questions.**

A seminar is a form of academic instruction, either at an academic institution or offered by a commercial or professional organization. It has the function of bringing together small groups for recurring meetings, focusing on some particular subject each time, in which everyone present is requested to participate. This is often accomplished through an ongoing Socratic dialogue with a seminar leader or instructor, or through a more formal presentation of research. It is essentially a place where assigned readings can be discussed, questions can be raised, and debates can be conducted.

1.   Is it OK for participants in a seminar to avoid speaking?

_____

2.   What do participants do to accomplish a seminar?

_____

3.   What preparations do participants have to make before the seminar?

_____

1.3 Think about what proper behavior would be in a seminar.

1.   Do you often keep silent in a seminar? What prevents students from participating in discussions? Two reasons are given below as examples. Work with your partner and add more reasons to the list.

Reasons:

e.g. I can't keep pace with other participants in the discussion.

    I'm nervous about speaking in front of other people.

_____

_____

_____

2.   What are your suggestions about behaving properly in a seminar?

Suggestions:

_____

_____

_____

3.   What do you think makes an effective seminar?

_____

_____

_____

Extensive Reading

At North American universities, the term "seminar" refers to a course of intense study relating to the student's major. In some European universities, a seminar may be a large lecture course, especially when conducted by a renowned thinker (regardless of the size of the audience or the scope of student participation in discussion). The idea behind the seminar system is to familiarize students more extensively with the methodology of their chosen subject and also to allow them to interact with examples of the practical problems that always occur during research work.

Section 2

Listening Attentively

A seminar is not only an important form of academic instruction in college education, but also a common class-like meeting, in which participants discuss a particular subject presented by one or several major speakers. That is, a seminar is made up of a lecture plus a follow-up discussion. In this sense, listening attentively to understand others' presentations is essential to join in a group discussion.

2.1 Listen to a radio program entitled *Technology Report* and take notes on what IBM researchers hope the computer chip TrueNorth to do in the future.

1. TrueNorth can program _____

    and then _____.

2. It can be used as _____.

3. It can also be used for _____

    _____

    and then _____.

2.2 **Suppose you are going to listen to a lecture entitled "How to Transform Apocalypse Fatigue into Action on Global Warming". Try to anticipate what it is about. Then answer the following questions. You can scan the bar code to know more about the background knowledge.**

1. What is the meaning of apocalypse? If you are not sure, consult it in the dictionary.

   _____

   _____

   _____

2. Do you know some causes of global warming?

   _____

   _____

   _____

3. What are the effects of global warming?

   _____

   _____

   _____

4. How can we treat global warming?

   _____

   _____

   _____

5. What have you known about global warming?

   _____

   _____

   _____

2.3 **You are going to listen to a lecture entitled "100 Solutions to Reverse Global Warming". Make some predictions to prepare for the listening.**

Tips

Predicting is an essential listening skill, which enables listeners to anticipate what they are going to hear. Predicting before the lecture ensures you an effective listener.

1. What is the topic of the lecture?

   _____

2. What can you infer from the title of the lecture as to the lecturer's attitude toward the effect of global warming? Is it a positive attitude or a negative one?

   _____

   _____

3. Work with your partner and make a list of solutions to global warming. Then listen to the lecture and see how many of your solutions are confirmed. Put a tick "√" in the appropriate box.

Potential Solutions	Confirmed	Not Confirmed

2.4 Read the following lecture titles. Choose one of them and predict what it is about.

- Averting the Climate Crisis
- Global Priorities Bigger than Climate Change

1. Think about at least three questions that you suppose will be dealt with in the lecture you have chosen.

   _____

   _____

   _____

2. Listen to the lecture you have chosen. Confirm or revise your prediction by checking if your questions are answered. Report whether you have made the correct prediction. Follow the steps below:

    - Repeat your prediction.
    - Report whether any of your prediction is confirmed.
    - Report whether you have revised your prediction while listening.

Section 3 / Understanding a Lecture

Oral presentation consists of introduction, body, and conclusion. The speaker would deliver the presentation from introduction to conclusion. In this sense, while listening to a lecture, we may try to identify the information in each part. Signposts are used to help listeners follow the presentation, as discussed in Chapter 3; in turn, listeners may catch the signposts to understand what speakers are doing in their speeches.

3.1 Listen to the first part of the passage "Academic Listening (1)". Then answer the following questions.

1. According to Susan, why are lectures the most daunting aspect of the university life?

    _____

    _____

2. According to Simon Williams, what is the benefit for students to attend a lecture?

_____

_____

3. What might be the purpose of a lecture?

_____

_____

4. Why do the two students think lectures are difficult to understand?

_____

_____

5. According to Christine Reeves, what is the most difficult in listening to lectures?

_____

_____

3.2 Discuss with your partner over the problems that might make it difficult for you to understand a lecture in English. You are encouraged to check whether you have the following potential problems or not and come up with more ideas.

Potential Problems	Yes or No?
Speakers' strong accent	
My lack of vocabulary	
My lack of proficiency	
Speed of delivery	
Complicated contents	
Unfamiliar topic	
Other Problems:	

_____

_____

_____

3.3 Exchange with your partner about the solutions to help us through the lectures.

Solutions:

_____

_____

_____

3.4 Listen to the second part of the passage "Academic Listening (1)". Then answer the following questions.

1. What are the clues in the lecture that may guide the audience?

_____

_____

2. How does the speaker use intonation in different situations?

Different Situations	Intonation Clues
The speaker has finished one idea.	
The speaker will move on to the next point.	
The speaker stresses an important point.	

3. What marker phrases are used to indicate the last point of the lecture?

_____

_____

4. How does the speaker make his question prominent at the end of the lecture?

_____

_____

3.5 Listen to the passage "Academic Listening (2)". Then answer the following questions.

1. What should the lecturer do at the end of the lecture according to Simon Williams?

_____

_____

_____

2. Why does Simon Williams say that a good lecturer would talk about what he was not able to do during his lecture?

_____

_____

_____

3. According to the audio clip, is it difficult for listeners to know the lecturers have reached their conclusion? Why or why not?

_____

_____

_____

4. What conclusion does Susan draw about how to understand lectures? Which do you think is the most useful?

_____

_____

_____

3.6 Read the following introductions of two lectures to your partner and ask him or her to figure out what problem the lecturers intend to address in the lectures.

Lecture 1: In the year 1901, a woman called Auguste was taken to a medical asylum in Frankfurt. Auguste was delusional and couldn't remember even the most basic details of her life. Her doctor was called Alois. Alois didn't know how to help Auguste, but he watched over her until, sadly, she passed away in 1906. After she died, Alois performed an autopsy and found strange plaques and tangles in Auguste's brain—the likes of which he had never seen before.

Problem: _____

_____

Lecture 2: How do you explain when things don't go as we assume? Or better, how do you explain when others are able to achieve things that seem to defy all of the assumptions? For example, why is Apple so innovative? Year after year, it's more innovative than all the competitors. And yet, it's just a computer company. It's just like everyone else. It has the same access to the same talent, the same agencies, the same consultants, the same media. Then why is it that Apple seems to have something different? Why is it that Martin Luther King led the Civil Rights Movement? He wasn't the only man who suffered in pre-Civil Rights America, and he certainly wasn't the only great orator of the day. Why him? And why is it that the Wright brothers were able to figure out controlled, man-powered flight when there were certainly other teams who were better qualified, better funded—and they didn't achieve man-powered flight, but the Wright brothers beat them at it. There's something else at play here.

Problem: _____

_____

3.7 Listen to the lecture "The Secrets of Spider Venom". Then fulfill the tasks.

1. Try to catch the major contents of the lecture. Are there any signposts used by the speaker that help you focus on certain points?

Items	Contents	Signposts
Topic		
Title		
Thesis		
Main Point 1		
Main Point 2		
Main Point 3		

(Continued)

Items	Contents	Signposts
Main Point 4		
Conclusion		

2. Exchange with your partner about what you have heard.

3. Read the lecture transcript to see whether you have understood all the main points.

7 Chapter

Supporting Your Views

Warm-up Questions:

1. What examples can illustrate "WeChat is now more popular than SMS in sending messages"?

2. If you have no ideas about the statement above, where do you think you can find proper materials?

To be academically convincing, our viewpoints need to be well supported by adequate and specific information, such as examples, reasons, and explanations in different ways. Efficient support is even more difficult than creating an idea. The ability to integrate and develop ideas from your reading is an essential aspect of academic life.

Section 1

Providing Further Information

1.1 Work in pairs on the topic "smartphones". Then fulfill the tasks.

1. Exchange your presentation outline with your partner.

Introduction	Topic:
	Thesis:
	Outline of contents:
Body (Main Points)	Point 1:
	Point 2:
	Point 3:
Conclusion	Summary:

2. After listening, give your questions or comments on the outline.

> Questions or Comments :
> e.g. I think the third point is less relevant to your argument.
> _____
> _____

3. Think about how you will support your main points.

_____

1.2 Work in groups. Read the news report "Will Robots Cost Us Our Jobs?". Then fulfill the tasks.

1. Prepare a summary of the main points about the influence of AI on people's jobs. Provide further information for each main point.

Overview:	
Main Points:	Supporting Information:
_____	_____
— _____	_____
_____	_____ _____

2. Present your summary in your group. Other students should give some feedback to the presentation in terms of the following factors.

Factors	Feedback
Volume	e.g. You should raise your voice at main points.
Speed	
Pause	
Intonation	
Pronunciation	
Eye Contact	
Posture	
Signposts	

3. Improve your summary based on the feedback and then present it to the class.

1.3 To convince listeners, you should have your viewpoints supported by adequate evidence. The support can be different kinds of information.

1. Look at how the familiar statement "Smoking is harmful to our health" is strongly supported in the left column. Then choose a kind of information in the box to fill in the form below.

| specific example | common sense | statistics | expert opinion |

Evidence	Kinds of Information
Roy didn't think he would ever suffer from any smoking-related illnesses. The doctor first told him he had heart disease: His arteries were clogged around his heart, causing hypertension and starving his heart for blood. But after the heart disease and before the heart attack, there was also the stroke that caused brain damage with resulting in partial paralysis to the right side of his body. Ugh. Life was no fun after that.	
It's common knowledge that lung cancer is closely related to smoking.	
A 2015 survey on Chinese adults' use of tobacco showed that China's smoking population increased by 15 million to 316 million compared with five years ago. The non-smoking population of 740 million is suffering from the second-hand smoke and about 1.4 million die from tobacco-related diseases every year.	
Zhi Xiuyi, director of the Lung Cancer Diagnosis and Treatment Center affiliated to the Capital Medical University, showed a range of data: In 2015, 733,000 people were diagnosed with lung cancer and 610,000 patients died from lung cancer. In addition, more than 70% of lung cancer patients were diagnosed at a late stage, losing the chance for curative treatment.	

2. Think about where we can manage to find such strong support for our own opinions.

Section 2

Reading into Thinking

2.1 Read the following statements. Then fulfill the tasks.

1. Choose two of them and think about how you will support them with efficient details.
    Try to use the different kinds of information discussed in 1.3.

    • A ride-hailing app is very convenient.
    • E-pay will replace cash.
    • Internet distracts the youth from Chinese Spring Festival gala.

2. Work in groups and tell your support to the others.

3. While listening to each other, think about whether you have supported your viewpoints
    efficiently. The following questions are designed for your evaluation.

(1) Does the speaker agree or disagree with the statement?

_____

_____

_____

(2) What are the reasons?

_____

_____

_____

(3) Do you think the presentation is convincing enough? Why or why not?

_____

_____

_____

(4) Present your viewpoints to the class.

_____

_____

_____

2.2 **Do you approve of the second-child policy? Work in three groups. Group 1 read Articles 1–4, Group 2 read Article 5 and Group 3 read the last one. Read them to see whether you will find evidence to support your view or you would like to change your opinion.**

1. I would like to support my view with the information in Article(s) _____. That is,

    _____

    _____

    _____.

2. I would like to change my opinion because the information in Article(s) _____ is more convincing. That is, _____

    _____

    _____.

Section 3

Quoting into Thinking

3.1 **Discuss with your partner about the secrets to success.**

Secrets to Success:

_____

_____

_____

3.2 Read the following quotations about the secrets to success. Then fulfill the tasks.

a. Don't let the noise of other opinions drown your own inner voice. And most importantly, have the courage to follow your heart and intuition; they somehow already know what you truly want to become. Everything else is secondary. (Steve Jobs)

b. The great successful men of the world have used their imagination...they think ahead and create their mental picture in all its details, filling in here, adding a little there, altering this a bit and that a bit, but steadily building—steadily building. (Robert Collier)

c. It takes 20 years to make an overnight success. (Eddie Cantor)

d. Never mind what others do; do better than yourself, beat your own record from day to day, and you are a success. (William J. H. Boetcker)

e. Success is not the result of spontaneous combustion. You must set yourself on fire. (Reggie Leach)

f. The secret of success in life is for a man to be ready for his opportunity when it comes. (Benjamin Disraeli)

g. Self-trust is the first secret of success. (Ralph Waldo Emerson)

h. All successful people, men and women, are big dreamers. They imagine what their future could be, ideal in every respect, and then they work every day toward their distant vision, that goal or purpose. (Brian Tracy)

i. The difference between a successful person and others is not a lack of strength, not a lack of knowledge, but rather a lack of will. (Vincent T. Lombardi)

j. The most successful people in life are generally those who have the best information. (Benjamin Disraeli)

1. Answer the following questions.

(1) Which statement comes closest to your belief about the secrets to success?

_____

(2) Which statements have the same implication?

_____

(3) Which statements seem to contradict one another?

_____

2. Report your view about the secrets to success. Support it with the quotations on the previous page. Besides, give an example of a person who succeeds because of the factors you attach importance to.

3.3 Work in pairs on the question "Is it worth going to college?". You and your partner should have opposing views. Support your views with the evidence from the articles about college education.

1. Yes, I believe it is worth going to college. _____

_____

_____

_____

2. No, I don't believe in this. _____

_____

_____

_____

3.4 The following sentences about the importance of going to college come from the father in the American movie _Accepted_. What do you think of these sentences?

> Society has rules. The first rule is to go to college.
> If you want to have a happy and successful life, you go to college.
> If you want to be somebody, you go to college.
> If you want to fit in, you go to college.

3.5 Discuss with your partner about some successful people who are college dropouts or even don't go to college.

1. Make a list of such people in China and in foreign countries. Share the stories of such people.

    _____

    _____

    _____

2. Do you think higher education and degrees are essential for one's success? Work with your partner and make a presentation on the value of college education.

    _____

    _____

    _____

8
Chapter

Leading a Seminar

1. Have you noticed the activities of a chairperson in a lecture or a seminar?

2. Imagine you are the chairperson of a group discussion in class. What will you say at the beginning and at the end respectively? How will you respond if the group members argue with each other?

To chair a seminar or a group discussion is part of our academic abilities. To keep the time of the presentation, to control the discussion, and to balance the disputes ensure that every participant has a chance to express his or her opinion and the discussion always sticks to the given topic. Thus the seminar will be a success.

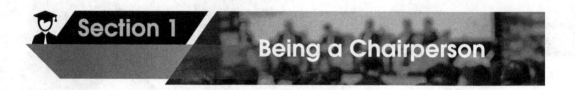

Section 1 / Being a Chairperson

1.1 Read the course requirements for the philosophy of science below. Then identify the different requirements for participants of different backgrounds.

Course Requirements

All participants are expected to do the assigned reading and to attend all the seminar sessions. There are two options for students taking this seminar for grades:

Option 1: Those students without significant background in philosophy of science may take the seminar as a regular course. This will require writing weekly discussion comments and three papers between 1,200 and 1,800 words based on the material we cover in class. The discussion comments, involving a paragraph commenting or raising a question about a major point in the assigned reading, must be submitted to the e-mail list (see below) by 11 a.m. prior to each seminar session. The three papers will be due on October 17, November 14, and December 8—these dates don't correspond to seminar dates. They should be submitted electronically in Microsoft Word to papers@mechanism.ucsd.edu.

Option 2: Those students with significant background in philosophy of science are encouraged to pursue the research option. This option will be directed toward preparing a paper to be submitted for publication. This will require picking a topic at the beginning of the course, leading a seminar session on relevant readings, and then presenting their own paper later in the seminar.

1. What are the students without background in philosophy required to do in their discussion comments?

    _____

    _____

    _____

2. Higher requirements fall on the students with background in philosophy in that they have to _____

    _____

    _____

    before the submission of their final papers.

3. What preparations do you think the students with background in philosophy should make before leading a seminar session?

    _____

    _____

    _____

1.2 Watch the video about Asian leadership by Nicholas Tse. Then answer the following questions.

1. Who introduces the keynote speaker Nicholas Tse?

    _____

    _____

2. What are the roles of an MC?

    _____

    _____

3. What does the headmaster talk about?

    _____

    _____

4. What does the moderator do to control the question and answer session?

    _____

    _____

5.　Can you now summarize the roles of a chairperson in a seminar?

_____

_____

1.3 Watch the video again and figure out the rules the MC announces. Practice announcing the rules like an MC.

1.　Firstly, _____

2.　Secondly, _____

3.　Thirdly, _____

4.　Last but not least, _____

1.4 Read the arrangements of conferences below. Then fulfill the tasks.

- **Session Format 1:** Full paper sessions are organized into 105-minute time blocks with no more than six papers per session. Each presenter will have 15–20 minutes, including time for questions and discussion. Keynote sessions are organized into 50-minute time blocks with no more than two papers per session.
- **Session Format 2:** In a presentation panel format, the moderator introduces each speaker and puts each talk in perspective. Each speaker gives a 15- or 20-minute prepared presentation. The moderator asks questions and elicits responses from the audience.
- **Session Format 3:** Two formats have traditionally prevailed at our Congress. At first, a main speaker talks for about 30 minutes, followed by a 15-minute commentary and a number of shorter statements of opinions; the rest of the time would be given over to general discussion. An alternative format involves three 20-minute papers on different aspects of the theme, then to be followed by general discussion.
- **Session Format 4:** The Exhibitors Hall will be available on Monday, Tuesday, Wednesday, and Thursday from 11:30 a.m. to 1:45 p.m. Time will be allocated to companies in one-hour time blocks on a first-come, first-served basis. A company may request one or two hours. Sessions will be scheduled from 11:30 a.m. to 12:30 p.m., and from 12:45 p.m. to 1:45 p.m. each day. Each one-hour time slot should include time for Q & A.

1. Work in pairs. Figure out what is arranged in different conferences and then complete the form below.

Formats	Sessions	Total Speakers	Time for Each Speaker	Question/Discussion: Followed/Included?
1	Keynote Session			
	Paper Session			
2				
3	Keynote Session			
	Paper Session			
4	Exhibition			

2. Look at the form above and practice announcing the arrangements of the conference as a chairperson. Remember to use your own words.

Section 2　Controlling the Discussion

2.1 Watch the video clip of *The Big Bang Theory* (Episode 13, Season 4). Notice how Sheldon deals with the conflicts among the speakers.

1. What does he say to dissolve the arguments between Miss Rostenkowski and Mr. Wolowitz?

_____

_____

_____

2. What does he say when Penny weighs in the discussion?

_____

_____

_____

3. What does he say when he thinks the speakers are shifting away from the topic?

_____

_____

_____

4. Do you think he is successful in chairing the conference? Why or why not?

_____

_____

_____

5. Do you have other ways to moderate the speakers who have different ideas in the conference?

_____

_____

_____

 Useful Expressions

How to Moderate the Disputes

- Well, Prof. XXX, I'm afraid that we have gone too far from our main theme. Let's come back.
- I think it's a good time to go on to the next question.
- Since we don't seem to be able to resolve this difference now, could we move on to the next point?
- Due to the time limitation, I would suggest that we discuss today's problem again in our next session.
- What do others think regarding the points debated by Mr. XXX and Mr. XXX?
- That's an interesting point. Mr. XXX, thank you.

2.2 Watch the question and answer session in the video clip about Asian leadership by Nicholas Tse. Then fulfill the tasks.

1. Notice what the moderator does to control the question and answer session. Some roles are listed below.

Roles of the Moderator	Sentence Numbers
Announcing the beginning of Q & A session	
Inviting questions from the audience	
Inviting answers from the speaker	
Reminding participants of time	
Reminding participants of topic	
Reminding participants of arrangements and rules	
Announcing the closing	

2. Then discuss with your partner which sentences in the following transcript match the roles in the form. Put the letters into the form above.

> a. Thank you for really encouraging our students to pursue our own dreams, our passions, and although we've asked quite a few questions, I'm sure the audience here have many more questions to ask you. So, we will now give the question to the floor.
>
> b. Just as a reminder, today's section is focused on entrepreneurship, leadership. This is important, so questions fall out of these categories will not be entertained.
>
> c. Originally, we have about 20 minutes for the Q & A section, so keep your questions brief and to the point. If they drag on for too long, I'm sorry but I'm gonna cut you short and I'm gonna get the questions from some other students, so please be respectful to the audience.
>
> d. Just another thing: When we hand you the microphone after asking a question, please pass it back to the staff members, so other people can get a chance. Thank you for your attention and we will now start taking questions.
>
> e. Sorry, we'll only have time for about two more questions. The lady in the front row there.
>
> f. Our last question will go to the guy in the black shirt.

g. Our last question will go to president Tony Qian. Will you do the honors?

h. Sorry, sorry, I won't entertain this, but I don't know if he is feeling generous?

i. That officially ends the Q & A session, Karen, back to you.

2.3 Have a discussion in groups on the topic "What does happiness mean to you?".

1. Take notes of the opinions given by all the other group members. Observe their behavior as well.

Opinions	Arguments
In my opinion, happiness means:	Because:

2. Make comments on their behavior based on the following questions.

- Does anyone keep silent?
- Does anyone give a lot of reasons?
- Does anyone talk for a long time?
- Does anyone give several opinions?

Comments:

_____

_____

_____

_____

3.   Make a group discussion about dealing with different situations as a chairperson.

Situations	What Could a Chairperson Say?
The discussion begins.	
Someone dominates the discussion.	
Someone doesn't say anything.	
No one speaks.	
Someone states his opinion but gives no argument.	
Someone wanders off the topic.	
Someone gives a complicated argument.	
The discussion comes to an end.	

2.4 Work in a group of five students, one chairperson and four participants. Simulate a seminar on the topic "What does happiness mean to you?".

1.   One participant first presents his or her opinion on happiness in two minutes and then the other participants make a discussion.

2.   The chairperson presides the discussion.

3.   When the discussion finishes, participants make comments on the chairperson's behavior. Does he or she control the discussion well? In what aspects does he or she perform well? What else can he or she do to perform better? Put a click "√" in the appropriate box (1=bad; 2=just so so; 3=good).

Chairperson's Behavior	1	2	3
Announcing the opening			
Introducing the topic			
Keeping the allocated time			
Calling on participation			
Moderating disputes			
Controlling the discussion			
Summarizing the discussion			
Thanking the speakers			
Declaring the closing			

4. Write down suggestions for improving the chairperson's behavior.

Suggestions:

_____

_____

_____

 Useful Expressions

How to Call on Participants

- Ladies and gentlemen, Dr. Li has now finished his speech. Are there any questions about his talk?
- May I ask if there are any questions for the speaker?
- Is there anyone else who wants to say something regarding Dr. Li's speech?
- Has anyone got anything to add to Dr. Li's presentation?
- Mr. Wang, could you please tell us what you think about it?

9
Chapter

Group Discussions

1. What are the differences between a seminar and a group discussion?

2. In what aspects are they similar?

Group discussions are not strange to graduate students. But they might be perplexed about how to build on others' opinions in order to proceed with their own points of view. Therefore, it is necessary to practice exchanging information and expressing agreement or disagreement, as well as to know some basic techniques to be an effective participant.

Section 1 **Participating in Group Discussions**

1.1 Discuss the following questions with your partner.

1. In what situations are you required to participate in a group discussion? Make a list as long as possible.

   _____

   _____

   _____

2. What might be the purpose of a group discussion in a certain situation?

   _____

   _____

   _____

3. Have you got any experience of a group discussion? If yes, have you managed to get to an agreement or not?

   _____

   _____

   _____

4. What preparations do you think are necessary for a group discussion?

   _____

   _____

   _____

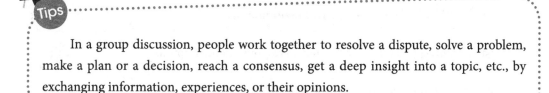

Tips

In a group discussion, people work together to resolve a dispute, solve a problem, make a plan or a decision, reach a consensus, get a deep insight into a topic, etc., by exchanging information, experiences, or their opinions.

1.2 Listen to a radio program entitled *9 Techniques for Effective Group Discussion*. Then fulfill the tasks.

Mayur from India asks: "I will have to face interviews and group discussions in order to get recruited into a company. Can you please tell me how to speak effectively in a group discussion?"

Catherine Chapman from BBC answers his question by suggesting nine techniques that can make him an effective participant.

1.   Listen to her suggestions and write down the nine techniques exactly.

(1) _____

(2) _____

(3) _____

(4) _____

(5) _____

(6) _____

(7) _____

(8) _____

(9) _____

2.   What is the most impressive technique to you? Write it down in your own words and then illustrate it to your partner.

_____

_____

3.   Listen to the radio program again. Then read the following statements and decide whether it is proper in a group discussion.

Behavior in Group Discussions	Proper or Not?
I listen attentively to others and make no response to their opinions.	
I am active in the discussion by speaking a lot.	
After I express my own idea, I hope to listen to others' opinions.	
I always speak briefly about my point to save time for others.	
We interrupt each other politely whenever we have a different idea.	
I don't take notes since different ideas emerge abundantly.	
I argue with other participants until they submit to my opinion.	

1.3 Watch the video clip of *The Big Bang Theory* (Episode 13, Season 4). Then answer the following questions.

1. What is supposed to be the topic of the seminar?

   _____

2. How many different ideas do the speakers have? Do they come to a consensus at the end?

   _____

   _____

   _____

3. What expressions are used to indicate "disagreement"?

   _____

   _____

   _____

Section 2 　 Exchanging Information

2.1 Work in pairs. One reads Article 1 and the other reads Article 2. Both should summarize the reasons for overseas study. Then exchange your information with the partner.

1. Follow the example below. Then change your roles.

    Student A: (Summary). Do you understand what I mean?

    Student B: If I have understood you correctly, you mean…

2. Think about what you will say if you don't follow the speaker.

2.2 Express the advantages or disadvantages of studying overseas to your partner and reach an agreement.

1. Discuss with your partner about the expressions for clarification. Follow the example below. Then change your roles.

    Student A: (Illustrations). _____?

    Student B: Well, I think…

2. Think about what you will say if you don't understand what your partner says. You can follow the useful expressions below.

Useful Expressions

How to Ask for Clarification

- I'm sorry, but could you repeat what you said about / but I'm not quite clear on…
- Could you be more specific about…?
- Could you expand a little bit on what you said about…? / Could you give an example of…?
- Could you explain it in more detail?

2.3 Watch the video clip of *The Big Bang Theory* (Episode 3, Season 2). Then answer the questions below.

1. What does Leonard think is the reason for Penny's addiction?

   _____

   _____

2. What does Dr. Winkle think of Penny's problem? What is her argument?

   _____

   _____

3. Does Leonard agree with Dr. Winkle? What does he respond to Dr. Winkle?

   _____

   _____

4. What does Sheldon think of Dr. Winkle's opinion?

   _____

   _____

5. What conclusion does Sheldon come to?

   _____

   _____

Section 3 / Expressing Agreement and Disagreement

3.1 Listen to the passage "Agreement and Disagreement". Then fulfill the tasks.

1. Work with your partner and try to catch the expressions for agreement and disagreement.

Expressions for Agreement	Expressions for Disagreement

(Continued)

Expressions for Agreement	Expressions for Disagreement

2.   If you have more expressions, write them down.

More Expressions:

_____

_____   _____

_____

3.2 Practice using the expressions for agreement and disagreement.

1.   In groups, discuss the smartphone function you value most. One student is the chairperson who controls the discussion. Some roles of a chairperson are listed below.

- Let everyone introduce himself.
- Introduce the topic.
- Smooth over conflict.
- Ask people to back up their opinions.
- Ask people to be aware of differences in their arguments.
- Draw a conclusion.

2. The other group members express agreement or disagreement on the ideas they hear. Come to an agreement on the functions that your group thinks are the most often used among young people. List the top five functions.

> Top Five Smartphone Functions:
>
> _____
>
> _____
>
> _____
>
> _____
>
> _____

3. The chairperson encourages each member to express opinions and reasons and to interact with other members.

4. The chairperson has to report the results of the discussion to the class by following the useful expressions below.

Useful Expressions

How to Summarize a Discussion

- We finally all agreed that…
- After much consideration, we decided that…
- Unfortunately, we couldn't reach an agreement on…Some felt that…, while others…

3.3 Read the statements below. Then fulfill the tasks.

> - **Statement 1:** It is necessary to use animals as victims in medical experiment.
> - **Statement 2:** Artificial intelligence will endanger human beings in the long run.
> - **Statement 3:** Electronic books will replace traditionally printed books.
> - **Statement 4:** Shopping online is more convenient than shopping in traditional stores.
> - **Statement 5:** E-pay is not safe.
> - **Statement 6:** Depression is the most serious social problem.
> - **Statement 7:** Humanities are not as useful as sciences and engineering.

1. Do you agree (A), disagree (D), or partly agree (P) with each one?

2. Work in pairs. Choose one of the statements above and repeat it to your partner. Listen

to your partner to see how he or she responds appropriately and politely rather than directly saying yes or no. He or she will then give his or her own opinion and at least one supporting reason.

Statements	Your Partner's Opinions (A/D/P)	Expressions for Opinions	Supporting Reason(s)
1			
2			
3			
4			
5			
6			
7			

 Useful Expressions

How to Partly Agree with an Opinion

- I agree to some extent.
- I agree up to a point, but…
- You could say that, but…
- I can see how you might think that, but…
- I still have my doubts, but okay…
- If you put it that way, I suppose…
- With reservations, I'm going to accept that…

3.4 Read the articles about college education in groups. Then fulfill the tasks.

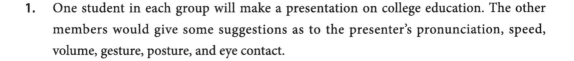

1. One student in each group will make a presentation on college education. The other members would give some suggestions as to the presenter's pronunciation, speed, volume, gesture, posture, and eye contact.

Speaker's Behavior	Suggestions
Pronunciation	
Speed	
Volume	
Gesture	
Posture	
Eye Contact	

2. The other students should scribble down the main points and the supporting details.

Presenter: _____

Topic: _____

Main Idea: _____

Main Points	Supporting Details
Point 1:	
Point 2:	
Point 3:	
Point 4:	
Point 5:	

3. In the follow-up group discussion, the chairperson tries to elicit everyone's opinion on the topic. They have to tell what points they agree with and what points they disagree with. Use the useful expressions discussed in 3.3 to show agreement or disagreement. Remember to give reasons for their statements.

Main Points	Agree/Disagree	Expressions	Reasons
Point 1			
Point 2			
Point 3			
Point 4			
Point 5			

4. After various ideas are put forward, the chairperson has to report the results of the discussion from a collection of different ideas by considering the following questions.

(1) What have you talked about?

(2) How many participants are there in your group?

(3) What are their opinions on college education?

(4) Have you come to an agreement or ended up with a disagreement?

10 Chapter

Asking and Answering Questions

Warm-up Questions:

1. Have you asked any questions after listening to a lecture? Can you recall your questions?

2. What might make students unwilling to ask questions in lectures?

An oral presentation is conventionally followed by a question and answer section. However, it is not easy to ask good questions. It depends on how well the questioner has done about the research. On the other hand, it requires both careful preparation and impromptu intelligence to deal with questions in a satisfactory way.

Section 1 — Designing a Questionnaire

1.1 Search on the Internet for a questionnaire. Then answer the following questions.

1. What is the purpose of the questionnaire?

   _____

   _____

   _____

2. What personal information of the correspondents is required?

   _____

   _____

   _____

1.2 Work in groups to prepare a questionnaire. Then fulfill the tasks.

1. Imagine that you work with an international tour agency and you want to learn about people's plan to travel overseas during the Spring Festival. You may take the following factors in the box into consideration.

potential destinations	duration of stay	travelling budget
independent travel	a package tour	departure date
leisure tour	shopping tour	in-depth travel

2. Write down six to eight questions for the questionnaire.

Questions:

_____

_____

_____

_____

_____

_____

_____

_____

3. Exchange your questionnaire with that of another group. Evaluate that questionnaire in your group. Discuss the following questions.

(1) Has that group decided the aim of their questionnaire? (e.g. To determine how many overseas travelling routes should be provided during the Spring Festival.)

(2) What is the focus of their questionnaire? (e.g. How much money are people willing to spend on their overseas vacation?)

(3) Can the questions elicit the relevant information?

(4) Do you have any suggestions for improvement?

(5) Are there any questions that could be added?

4. Fill in the questionnaire from another group and return it. Make your comments on the questionnaire.

5. With the feedback from the other group, you can revise your own questionnaire.

A questionnaire is made up of a list of questions created by a person, organization, or company to find out people's opinions on a particular topic.

Closed-ended questions, like yes-or-no questions, true-or-false questions, or questions that ask for agreement or disagreement with a statement, are used to gather specific answers.

Open-ended questions, on the other hand, aim to solicit answers from correspondents and don't provide them with specific answers to choose from.

1.3 Each group member selects two or three questions in your questionnaire. Interview four students from other groups and write down their answers.

Questions	Correspondents' Responses

1.4 Make a generalization of their answers. Report your survey result to the class. The following is an example.

e.g. Approximately half of the correspondents claimed that they would like to spend their Spring Festival in Japan.

Section 2   **Making an Interview**

2.1 Watch the video clip about Asian leadership by Nicholas Tse. Then fulfill the tasks.

1.   In this part, Nicholas Tse is interviewed by three student representatives. What is the focus of the questions?

2.   Look at some questions in the interview.

> • **Q1:** And, we want to know what the greatest challenge is when you start up your company.
> • **Q2:** But now would you advise us about finding our dreams and our passions?
> • **Q3:** Then what do you think is the key leadership quality that is most important to success to you?
> • **Q4:** But now, so, for qualities of your employees, what's your specific quality of your employees you'll be looking for?
> • **Q5:** Working in creative media industry, I suppose there could be some divergent opinions amongst your work. When you actually face such type of situation, how would you settle those disagreements?
> • **Q6:** So, it is inevitable that there are ups and downs in our life. So, how do you stay positive?

3.   Watch this part again. Work in six groups, each responsible for one question. Try to catch the main points in Nicholas Tse's answers to the questions above.

4. In your group, exchange the main points you have heard from the five groups.

5. Report the results of your discussion. Two members in your group take the roles of the interviewer and Nicholas Tse respectively. Perform the interview to the class.

2.2 Practice interviewing celebrities.

1. Work in pairs. You are supposed to act as one of the celebrities below and will be interviewed by your partner who acts as a journalist working for the school newspaper. The journalist should prepare a list of questions beforehand and take notes during the interview.

- Ma Yun
- Yao Ming
- Bill Gates
- Mark Elliot Zuckerberg

Questions	Responses

2. The journalist then summarizes the main points from your answers and presents them from the third person's perspective.

2.3 Practice interviewing common people.

1. Interview the people who are eager to go home in the Spring Festival travel rush. Suppose you are a journalist from CCTV. Think about the difficulties facing those people.

Difficulties:
_____
_____
_____

2. Prepare some questions for your potential correspondents.

> Questions:
>
> _____
>
> _____
>
> _____

3. Work in groups. You may interview the other group members with the questions above. Then change your roles until every interviewer has finished asking the questions.

4. Collect the questions and answers. Select two or three inspiring questions and their answers. One member prepares to present the interview in front of the class and your presentation should include the following aspects:

- The purpose of the interview;
- Where the interview is conducted;
- What questions are used in the interview;
- How many people are interviewed;
- Answers from the correspondents.

2.4 Think about the questions you might face in job interviews.

1. Look at the top 10 job interview questions.

> - Tell me about yourself.
> - Why should we hire you?
> - What is your greatest strength?
> - What is your greatest weakness?
> - Why are you leaving or why have you left your job?

- What are your salary expectations?
- Why do you want this job?
- How do you handle stress and pressure?
- Describe a difficult work situation or project and how you overcame it.
- What are your goals for the future?

2. Answer two or three questions listed above. Discuss answers with your partner.

Questions	Your Answers

3. Read the article "Top 10 Job Interview Questions and Best Answers". Then revise your answers above.

4. Practice the job interview with your partner.

5. At the close of the interview, most interviewers ask whether you have any questions about the job or company. What questions do you want to ask the interviewers? Discuss with your partner and write them down.

Questions:

_____

_____

_____

Section 3

Defending Your Thesis

3.1 Work with your partner and come up with at least three questions that you may anticipate in your thesis defense.

Questions:

_____

_____

_____

3.2 Read the following three types of questions and the top 10 questions usually asked by the committee in thesis defense. Discuss with your partner which type these questions belong to. Match them with the three types of questions.

- **Type 1:** Probing Questions—The thesis defense committee would like you to broaden the thesis' most controversial aspects.
- **Type 2:** Curious Questions—The thesis defense committee would like you to give an overall view of the field under study and your contribution to it.
- **Type 3:** Hostile Questions—The thesis defense committee will expose an area of insufficiency.

Questions	Types of Questions
In one sentence, what is the main claim, point, or argument of your thesis?	
Why did you rely on Scholar X rather than Scholar Y? Why did you omit Theory Z? How did bringing together these two different disciplines enrich or limit your research?	
Please clarify what you mean by this statement on…	
How does your project contribute to knowledge in your field?	
How has your conception of this project changed over time?	
What have you learned about conducting research in this field?	
Were you unable to complete any aspect of this project as originally conceived?	
What part of the thesis did you enjoy most?	
What would you do differently if you had to do it all over again?	
Do you plan to continue this project?	

Section 4 / Asking and Answering Questions at a Seminar

4.1 Watch the video clip about Asian leadership by Nicholas Tse to see how questions are asked and answered.

1. In this part, students ask Nicholas Tse some questions. Listen to the questions attentively. A few of them are put here.

> • **Q1:** Hi, Nicholas, very nice to see you here. Actually we all know you as a very successful actor and singer…am I right…instead of being an entrepreneur. So, I just want to ask: How did your great fame affect your occupation, your business? Is there any negative effect? Because there must be some negative effects. Thank you very much.
>
> • **Q4:** Hi! You have mentioned about the challenges your company had before. How about the great success of your company?
>
> • **Q11:** Hi, Nicholas, my name is Ken. As you mentioned the skill of post-production in Hong Kong is not that far from the Western industry. The only difference is in terms of culture. So I want to ask: Do you have any plans to bring the post-production office to the international market by overcoming this barrier?

2. Underline the sentences in the box above that show what the students do before they ask the questions.

3. Nicholas Tse answers every question friendly. Underline the sentences in the box below that show his kindness to the questioners.

> • **Nicholas:** That is an awesome question! You know, I was gonna say about the category that the questions are gonna come by. I was gonna say if anyone was gonna asking for an autograph. I would sign you the autograph if you can ask me a question that was a starter. Because after all we're all in the study of MBA. Why not study in negotiating? But I like that question…yes, I didn't launch to the public that I had this company, that I have this company until April 2 last…
>
> • **Nicholas:** I…I like that question, it's hard…I have a tendency of rush. As to all kids should, actually maybe when they're 22 or 23, right? We kind of rush into things.

And when I first started this business, I didn't go all the way to know it each and every part of department of how they run the business, or I had...I had the picture of it. But then it came to the part where I had to buy really expensive machinery. When I was buying the second-hand piece of a color-corrector, I did...

- **Nicholas:** Uh, it's a good question, really. I used to hate that shadow that overpowered Nicholas Tse, because I am the son of whom and whom. But I have learned maybe because I started working at the age of 15 or 16. And now, did my parents do anything wrong? I have learned to accept and actually be proud of who they are. I used to really hate that shadow...

4.2 Discuss the question with your partner: In what way do the questioners show their politeness in the following two questions?

- **Q1:** I'm very much interested in hearing your presentation today. Now, would you please say a few more words about the tentative assumptions? Particularly at its preliminary stage?
- **Q2:** Thank you very much for your patient explanation in response to my question. But I have one more question, or rather a request—can I have a copy of your report?

4.3 Match the questions with the behavior. Each question may reflect different behavior.

- **Q1:** I have a question for Dr. Johnson. You mentioned the application of robots in your experiment. I didn't really understand that. Could you explain that a little bit more?
- **Q2:** As you mentioned in your talk, you're conducting the experiments on extensive application of robots. I'm not specialized in the subject, but I'm sure it will involve a rather complicated technological process. Would you mind telling us more specific statistics about that?
- **Q3:** Perhaps we're looking at the problem from different viewpoints. To the best of my knowledge, what you say seems to be theoretically unclear. Could you give us further explanation on that aspect?

Questions	Behavior
Q1 _____	a. Ask questions directly.
	b. Repeat key points in the presentation.
Q2 _____	c. Ask for sensitive information.
	d. Ask questions in a roundabout way.
Q3 _____	e. Raise different opinions.
	f. Request to clarify a problem.

4.4 **Watch the video "How Tech Companies Deceive You into Giving up Your Data and Privacy". Then fulfill the tasks.**

1. Answer the following questions.

(1) How does the speaker begin with his speech?

_____

(2) In what way does the speaker achieve a good beginning?

_____

(3) Why is Cayla so popular?

_____

(4) According to the speaker, what is the danger of playing with Cayla?

_____

(5) What is the purpose of the speech?

_____

2. Prepare at least two questions for the speaker. Remember to ask questions in a polite and roundabout way.

> Questions:
>
> _____
>
> _____

3. Watch the video again. If necessary, look at the transcript of the video. Discuss with your partner about the answers to the questions above and write them down.

> Answers:
>
> _____
>
> _____

4. Take the roles of speaker and questioner respectively. In front of the class, you and your partner ask and answer the questions you have prepared.

11
Chapter

Thinking Critically

Academically, students are required to think critically and take an analytical approach to the given tasks. Being able to debate and argue a point is a valuable skill for critical thinking. Facing an opposite view, students should know how to compare it with others, rebut it, and find faults with it, besides supporting their own views with specific examples and facts.

Section 1 — Creating an Argument

1.1 Select one of the following two topics. Work with your partner to make an argument for or against it. Then answer the following questions.

Topic 1: Beijing, Shanghai, and Chengdu now allow visually impaired passengers to take guide dogs onto the subway. Should guide dogs be allowed on the subway?

1. What is your stand? Are you for or against it?

    _____

    _____

    _____

2. What are your reasons?

    _____

    _____

    _____

3.   Who would disagree with you?

_____

_____

_____

4.   What might be the reasons or arguments against yours?

_____

_____

_____

5.   What is your suggestion to solve the problems mentioned by the opposite side?

_____

_____

_____

Topic 2: Online chat wastes or saves time and money.

1.   What is your view on online chat?

_____

_____

_____

2.   How do you support your viewpoint?

_____

_____

_____

3.   What might be the reasons or arguments for the opposite stand?

_____

_____

_____

4.   What is your comment on these reasons or arguments?

_____

_____

_____

1.2 Present arguments for the two topics in 1.1 from different stands. While listening, other students should take notes of the main arguments.

Topics	Arguments for	Arguments Against
Topic 1: Guide dogs are allowed on the subway.		
Topic 2: Online chat saves time and money.		

1.3 Are you addicted to your smartphone? Read the following symptoms of smartphone addiction. Then fulfill the tasks.

Top 8 Symptoms

- You use it in the bathroom.
- You feel panic when groping to the bottom of your purse.
- When you meet people with the same phone, you can only talk about the phone.
- You broke it and it feels like you lost a friend.
- A full battery charge barely lasts a day.
- You've cut back on necessities to afford your monthly cell phone bill.
- You prefer spending time browsing the Internet over face-to-face social interaction.
- You have alarms telling you when to do everything in your life.

1. Work in a group of four or five students. Write a questionnaire with a list of questions that ask people's opinions about smartphone use.

Questions:

_____

_____

_____

_____

_____

_____

_____

_____

2. Interview other group members about their symptoms of smartphone addiction. Write down their responses. Put a tick "√" in the appropriate box (1=severely addicted; 2=moderately addicted; 3=slightly addicted; 4=not addicted).

Students	Symptoms	Responses	Addiction			
			1	2	3	4

3. One student gives an introduction to the survey that was conducted.

4. The other students present one or two of the questions that were asked, responses that were received, and interesting comments that were made by the students who were interviewed. The comments mentioned should help explain why they use their smartphones so often. The presentation may cover the following aspects:

- The number of students who have certain symptoms and the degree of their smartphone addiction;
- A generalization of their comments, reasons, or explanations as to their smartphone addiction (e.g. Why do they use their smartphones so often or what do they do continually on smartphones?).

5. The last student summarizes the findings from the survey and interprets them. The summary may cover the following aspects:

- Symptoms common to most students;
- A generalization of reasons.

6. Make a group discussion about solutions to smartphone addiction. A chairperson encourages the group members to give as many solutions as possible and presents the results of the discussion to the class.

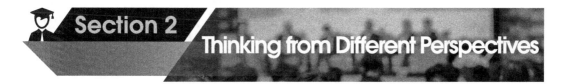

Section 2　Thinking from Different Perspectives

2.1 Work in groups on the topic about the second-child policy. Then fulfill the tasks.

1. Do you approve or disapprove of it? Write down your own idea and give your reasons.

   Your own idea: _____

   Reason(s): _____

   _____

2. The other members in the group will think about giving birth to a second child from the perspectives of the following people. Will they approve or disapprove of it? Conceive of an idea from their perspectives respectively. Support it with further information from Articles 1–6.

(1) Fathers:

   Idea:_____

   _____

   Reasons:_____

   _____

(2) Mothers:

   Idea:_____

   _____

   Reasons:_____

   _____

(3) Grandparents:

   Idea:_____

   _____

   Reasons:_____

   _____

(4) The first child of a family:

   Idea:_____

   _____

Reasons:_____

_____

(5) Sociologists:

Idea:_____

_____

Reasons:_____

_____

(6) Psychologists:

Idea:_____

_____

Reasons:_____

_____

3. Discuss your ideas with your group members, and give reasons. Use the following expressions in the box to show different perspectives.

 Useful Expressions

How to Show Different Perspectives

- From sociologists' perspective, …
- If I were the first child in the family, I would probably feel that…
- Grandparents would argue that…
- From the point of view of parents, …
- From my part, …

4. One student in your group need to report different perspectives on giving birth to a second child in front of the class.

2.2 Look at the following statements about education. Then fulfill the tasks.

- **Statement 1:** Sticks make sons.
- **Statement 2:** Home schooling is better than school education.
- **Statement 3:** High school students should be allowed to choose universities on their own.
- **Statement 4:** It is right for universities to lower academic standards to enroll students with special athletic or art abilities.

1. Consider each statement from the perspectives of different people who might be affected. How would they think of the statements? What are their reasons?

Statements	Different Perspectives and Reasons		
1	*Parents* would object to it since sticking would injure their children.		
2			
3			
4			

2. In groups, discuss one of the four statements above to see how many views from different people you can conceive of.

Section 3 / Making Contrast and Comparison

3.1 Skim the excerpt from the article "Rich Dad, Poor Dad". Then answer the following questions.

1. Which word is used repeatedly to mean the two dads when they are compared?

   _____

2. What signpost leads us to a contrast between the two dads?

   _____

3. What expression appears more than once when the two dads are contrasted?

   _____

4. What conclusion do the authors draw after the comparison and contrast?

   _____

3.2 Work in groups and make a comparison between Chinese dream and American dream.

American Dream:

- I have a dream that one day this nation will rise up and live out the true meaning of its creed that all men are created equal.

- The American dream is the belief that anyone, regardless of where they were born or what class they were born into, can attain their own version of success in a society where upward mobility is possible for everyone. The American dream is achieved through sacrifice, risk-taking, and hard work, rather than by chance.

- It is not a dream of motor cars and high wages merely, but a dream of social order in which each man and each woman shall be able to attain to the fullest stature of which they are innately capable, and be recognized by others for what they are, regardless of the fortuitous circumstances of birth or position.

Chinese Dream:

- Everyone has their own ideals, pursuits, and dreams. Everyone is also talking about the Chinese dream now. Since modern times, the greatest Chinese dream, I believe, has been to achieve the rejuvenation of the Chinese nation.
- To achieve the greatest dream means to achieve prosperity of the country, rejuvenation of the nation and happiness of the people.
- That all people, living in this great land and this great epoch, enjoy equal opportunities toward a colorful life, toward realization of their dreams.

1. Are there any similarities and differences between the two dreams? Discuss in groups and fulfill the form below.

Similarities	Differences

2. Give a presentation to the class on your group discussion results and your analysis. Follow the outline below.

- Introduction: greetings, topic, purpose, thesis, outline of the speech;
- Body: similarities, differences;
- Conclusion: summary.

3.3 Read the following list of environmental problems. Then fulfill the tasks.

- Global warming and the greenhouse effect;
- Acid deposition;
- Air pollution;
- Volcanic eruption;

- Drinking water pollution;
- Air pollution;
- Floods;
- Population growth.

1. Rank them in order from the most devastating to the least devastating. Discuss in groups and compare the rankings from other group members.

2. Present your ranking of the top three environmental problems and your reasons to the class. Follow the outline below.

   - Introduction: greetings, topic, purpose, thesis, outline of the speech;
   - Body: top three problems and your reasons;
   - Conclusion: summary.

Section 4   Debating

Debate is a formal method of interactive and representational arguments, commonly used in classrooms to strengthen students' leadership, interpersonal influence, and team work, besides oral presentation skills. In a debate, participants either argue for or against a given statement. For educational purpose, debates in classrooms train students in supporting their arguments and opposing the arguments of the other team.

4.1 Consider the differences between a seminar and a debate. Then fulfill the tasks.

• Combative in nature, objective to win.	• Cooperative in nature, objective to work together to understand and explore materials.
• Listen to find flaws in opponents' arguments; focus only on weaknesses and flaws in opponents' position; never acknowledge strengths.	• Listen critically to develop understanding and meaning; look for insights into others' ideas; examine both strengths and weaknesses.
• "Silence" others with the strength of your arguments and personality.	• Encourage everyone's participation; draw out reluctant participants.
• Defend assumptions.	• Explore assumptions.
• Attack others' ideas; exploit weaknesses.	• Support and build upon others' ideas; look for strengths in others' ideas to advance your own.

1. The sentences on the left column describe a _____ while those on the right column describe a _____.

2. Discuss with your partner and try to use your own words to describe the differences that impress you the most.

4.2 Solicit students' opinions about shared bikes. Then write down their answers.

Advantages	Disadvantages

4.3 **Eight students work in one group. Choose your stance as to the following statement and form two teams, one arguing for the statement while the other against it. Write down your names in order.**

Statement: Shared bikes have more advantages over disadvantages.	
Team for the Statement	Team Against the Statement
Speaker 1:	Speaker 1:
Speaker 2:	Speaker 2:
Speaker 3:	Speaker 3:
Speaker 4:	Speaker 4:

Each speaker in the two teams should present his or her opinion with strong enough evidence. You should follow the rules in the form and refer to the useful expressions.

Debate in Order	Useful Expressions
Speaker 1 (stating the basic standpoint in two minutes): For/Against	• We would like to introduce our stand that… • In order to effectively debate this topic, we would like to propose/elaborate / make clear that… • The main argument focuses on…
Speaker 2 (stating the basic standpoint and refuting the point of the first debater of the opposite team in two minutes):	• The other team has tried to make some good points; however, … • Their opinions may seem plausible at first glance; however, … • It is easy enough to make broad generalization about…like the other team just did, but in reality it is a very complex issue.
Speaker 3 (stating the basic standpoint and refuting the point of the second debater of the opposite team in two minutes):	(ibid.)

(Continued)

Debate in Order	Useful Expressions
Speaker 4 (summarizing the viewpoints and arguments of your side in two minutes):	• To conclude, we must emphasize our opinions of…; therefore, the other team's point of view can no longer be supported. • To sum up, our motion must stand, simply because during the debate we have shown…

4.4 Read the following five steps suggested by Chicago National Association for Urban Debate Leagues for first-year debaters. Then fulfill the tasks.

- **Step 1:** Refer back to the tag of your argument. This step is where you indicate to the judge what argument you want to extend. Make a specific reference to an earlier speech by your team where the argument was initiated. This could include a piece of evidence. This technique is often called "signposting".
- **Step 2:** Explain your argument. In this stage you comprehensively explain your argument. This step may take one sentence or several, depending on the time pressure in the speech and the importance of the argument. Explanations should include a statement of the underlying reasoning and proof for your claim.
- **Step 3:** Characterize your opponent's response to your argument. Your description should be fair. Don't be critical of the other side's argument. Don't call it "stupid" or "silly". You will lose credibility with the judge if you do that. This part should also be brief, but you do want to develop an understanding in the judge's mind.
- **Step 4:** Resolve the issue. At this stage you explain why you are right and they are wrong. It could be something as simple as pointing out that your evidence is more recent or qualified. Other ways to resolve the issue include: use of historical example, and a claim of a consensus viewpoint. The most common way to resolve an argument is to prove that your side contains internal logic that is not assumed by the other side's argument.
- **Step 5:** Impact the importance of winning the argument. The final step involves providing an impact assessment. You want to get maximum credit for winning the particular clash battle, so tell the judge what it is exactly that you win if they do resolve the issue in your favor.

Match the five steps above with the following sentences.

Sentences	Number of Steps
Our evidence is more recent than their evidence and comes from studies whereas their evidence is just one person's opinion.	
Statistics from all parts of the country indicate test scores are declining, and schools are literally falling apart.	
They say schools are getting better.	
Our third argument is that schools are getting worse.	
If we win this, it proves we win inherency, that status quo efforts are failing.	

4.5 Rebut the following statements. You can use the useful expressions in the box.

- Money means happiness. People are happy with a bunch of luxuries. Women in low spirits even console themselves by shopping. Obviously, money cures their sadness.
- Smartphones can replace PCs in functions. Nowadays, we surf the Internet, listen to music, watch videos, send and receive e-mails, and take photos. We can do more things on a smartphone than on a PC.
- Guide dogs should be allowed on public transportation. Beijing on Friday started allowing visually impaired passengers to take guide dogs onto the subway. The guide dogs may help visually impaired people to step into the world.
- Living on campus is a better choice than living off campus. It is convenient to transit from one class to another if we live on campus. In addition, campus facilities, like libraries, gyms, and computer centers, are easily accessible.

Useful Expressions

How to Rebut a Statement

- It is true that…, but…
- Proponents/Uplifters realize that…, yet they believe…
- Supporters recognize…, still they don't acknowledge…
- This is not to say that…, but to…
- …argues/claims that…, but…reveals/shows/indicates…
- In short, the opponents believe…because…However, …

4.6 Think about the faults with the arguments in the left column in the form below. Then state the faults with the claims in the right column.

Arguments	Faults
Secondly, capital punishment is useless, for it doesn't deter others from the same crime. （邹颉，2006）	Deterrence, obviously, is one of the aims of punishment, but it is surely not the only one.
Traditional ideas always believe, as people reach fifty, they have to face their increasingly serious age-related mental and physical deterioration. So they are not good for staying at work any longer. （辛斌，2008）	This is not always the case. Healthy and energetic people now routinely work through their 60s, even beyond, and remain dazzlingly productive.
Using torture as a punishment or to secure confessions disregards the rights of individuals. (Crusius & Carolyn, 1999)	Well, if life is so valuable that it must never be taken, the lives of innocents must be saved even at the price of hurting the one who endangers them.
Executing a murderer will not bring back his victim.	But torture, in the cases described, is intended not to bring anyone back but to keep innocents from being dispatched.
Torture is impermissible, a throwback to a more brutal age. (Crusius & Carolyn, 1999)	I believe this attitude is unwise. There are situations in which torture is not merely permissible but morally mandatory. Moreover, these situations are moving from the realm of imagination to fact.
Banning takeaway food into resident halls, we aim to cultivate students' social responsibilities.	However, I find no relation between the ban and responsibilities; instead, takeaway food saves us a lot of time and energy.

12 Chapter

Preparing for a Test

So far, you have learned some presentation skills and practiced speaking in different academic situations. Are you ready for a test? This chapter provides three topics for you to simulate a group discussion.

Seminar 1   Conquering Yourself

1.1 In 2018 Toastmaster International English Speech Contest, Sherrie Su from China delivered her speech "Turn Around". Watch the video and discuss the following questions with your partner.

1. What does Sherrie Su want to tell us in her speech?

2. What is the effect of talking about her own experience?

3. What do you learn from her stories?

4. How does she succeed in impressing the audience?

1.2 Make a presentation on the question "Turn your back on or turn around?". The presentation should focus on the answers to the questions below.

1. Have you got any experiences or problems that you want to turn your back on?

2. What can help us turn around to courageously face reality?

1.3 Work in groups and listen to one student's presentation on the topic above. Then fulfill the tasks.

1. Each member in a group makes comments on the presentation.

2. The chairperson in each group encourages the group members to participate in the discussion and reports the results of the discussion to the class.

Read the following news report from *China Daily*. Then fulfill the tasks.

1978–1988: New Look

A 1978 Japanese documentary, *China's New Look*, featured a scene that said everything about what the Chinese craved back then. In front of an old-fashioned television set, dozens of Shanghainese gathered around to watch a TV show.

In 1981, only one out of every 170 urban households in China had a color television. Having a TV set at home was something worth boasting about, especially when a man would propose.

As China started to open its doors to foreign manufacturers, a TV, a refrigerator, and a washing machine became a "must-have" home appliances set for a typical middle-class family.

"With more electronic products available, color televisions, cassette recorders, stereo components, record players, and electronic games and toys, which were only a dream just a decade ago, can now be found in millions of Chinese homes," read a Xinhua story in 1987.

1988–1998: West Meets East

In October 1990, the first outlet of McDonald's on the Chinese mainland opened for business in Shenzhen, a southern city at the forefront of China's opening-up.

The Western fast-food chain quickly became the hottest tourist spot in town. Curious Chinese consumers lined up in front of the 20 cashiers of the three-story building, shouting to the staff "I want 10 big macs", recalled a trainee with McDonald's at that time.

A meal at McDonald's was never so fast. China's new rich would line up at the fancy Western restaurant for two hours to chat with friends, discuss businesses, or even have a date.

While McDonald's stood for fashion, a Volkswagen's Santana car was a symbol for status. As many Chinese once said, somewhat jokingly: "As long as you have a Santana, you have nothing to fear driving all around the world."

The German automaker set up its first joint venture (JV) with SAIC Motor in Shanghai in 1985. By the end of 1991, the JV produced more than 100,000 Santana cars in total.

Following the success, Volkswagen has been expanding its footprint in China, with the establishment of a second venture, FAW Volkswagen, in northeastern city of Changchun in

1991, and a third in Hefei, eastern Anhui Province, in 2017.

1998–2008: Here Comes WTO

For many Chinese, the year 2001 was pretty unforgettable. The year marked the start of a new millennium and led to a whole new era as China joined the World Trade Organization (WTO).

From 2001 to 2017, China's average growth of imports in commodities and services was more than twice the world's average.

China never paused to open its market wider in fear of competition. In the spring of 2007, the 101st session of Canton Fair, China's oldest trade fair that dated back to 1957, set up a new section for imports—a signal that imports are no longer a "side dish" at China's trade events.

2008–2018: New Beginning

Shanghai, a city of long-time commercial culture, is always a step ahead in China's foreign trade.

In 2013, China established its first pilot Free Trade Zone (FTZ) in Shanghai's Pudong New Area and expanded to a larger area in Pudong in 2015. It was announced on November 5, the day the CIIE opened, that the Shanghai FTZ would expand further.

Preferential policies in the FTZ, including the negative list for foreign investment and the cross-border renminbi capital pool policy, effectively boosted the development of many multinational companies.

In 2010, the city hosted the 2010 World Expo, a milestone that showcased China's sincere wish to open to the world.

The Shanghai World Expo, the first held in a developing country in the event's 159-year history, set a record in terms of the number of participating countries or regions, the size of the Expo park, and the number of visitors.

With the successful hosting of China's first import expo, the city continued to drive China's import agenda. As China pledged further opening-up, this gathering will be remembered as a new beginning for China's import history.

1. Do more research on the great changes in China since the reform and opening-up in 1978.

2. Make a group discussion about the following questions.

(1) What other great changes do you know about China?

(2) What changes do you think have greatly influenced your life?

(3) What changes do you think will make our life different in the near future?

(4) What changes do you eagerly expect to appear?

3. Each member in a group expresses his or her opinion and makes comments on the

changes put forward by the other members.

4. The chairperson in each group encourages the group members to participate in the discussion and guides the discussion into an agreement on top five great changes in China. Finally the chairperson reports the results of the discussion to the class.

Seminar 3 / Transgenic Food Safety

Read the following news report from *China Daily*. Then fulfill the tasks.

Chinese Academician: Transgenic Food Is Safe

"Transgenic food is safe," said Shi Yuanchun, academician of both the Chinese Academy of Sciences and Chinese Academy of Engineering, in Beijing on June 4.

The dispute between the United States and the European Union on transgenic food mainly focuses on trade issues instead of technologic issues.

Shi made the remarks in response to a question at the Seventh General Assembly of the Chinese Academy of Engineering, saying that organisms in common food are naturally selected, while genes of transgenic food are reassembled through science and technology and no risks exist.

"People's worries about transgenic food stay focused on food allergies and gene flow," he acknowledged.

"More than 1,000 transgenic foods are sold in the U.S. supermarkets and no case related to food allergies or other transgenic problems occurred," he said.

"So far, the problem of gene flow has not happened in the world, although gene flow is possible theoretically," he acknowledged, adding that this issue can be resolved completely with the development of science.

"The crucial discovery of DNA and genetic technology creates opportunities for China's agricultural development," he said, noting that China should take this opportunity to develop biological research and industry, which is a vital strategy of agricultural development of China.

1. Do more research on transgenic food in a group.

2. Give a presentation on the safety of transgenic food.

3. Each member in a group makes comments on the presentation.

4. The chairperson in each group encourages the group members to participate in the discussion and reports the results of the discussion to the class.

Bibliography

Crusius, T. W., & Carolyn, E. C. (1999). *The aims of argument: A brief rhetoric.* California: Mayfield Publishing Company.

蔡基刚 . 2012. 学术英语 . 北京：外语教学与研究出版社 .

陈美华 . 2013. 学术交流英语 . 北京：外语教学与研究出版社 .

胡庚申 . 2013. 国际会议交流 . 北京：外语教学与研究出版社 .

辛斌 . 2008. 研究生英语读与写 . 上海：复旦大学出版社 .

邹颉 . 2006. 高级英语 . 杭州：浙江大学出版社 .

西安电子科技大学 | 人工智能学院
XIDIAN UNIVERSITY | College of Artificial Intelligence

理论性、实践性与创新性相结合，注重趣味性，极具实操性

人工智能实验
简明教程

焦李成 孙其功 田小林 侯彪 李阳阳 编著
Jiao Licheng　Sun Qigong　Tian Xiaolin　Hou Biao　Li Yangyang

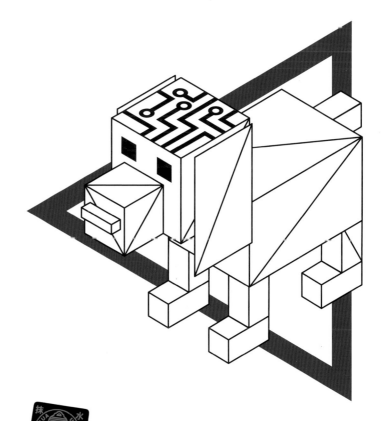

ARTIFICIAL

INTELLIGENCE

EXPERIMENTS TUTORIAL

清华大学出版社

图 2.1　黑白照片上色

（图片来自 N 软网 IT 资讯）

图 2.2　开国大典原图

（图片来自开国大典影像档案）

图 2.3　开国大典修复后图片

（图片来自电影《决胜时刻》）

图 2.12　修复前后对比图

图 3.1　图片修复效果

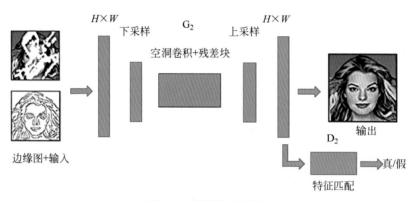

图 3.8　图像补全网络

图 3.12　缺失图像展示

图 3.13 补全效果图展示

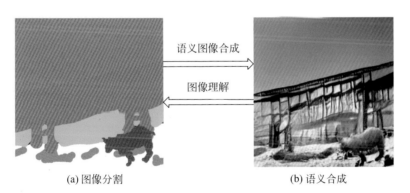

(a) 图像分割   (b) 语义合成

图 4.2 语义图合成原理图

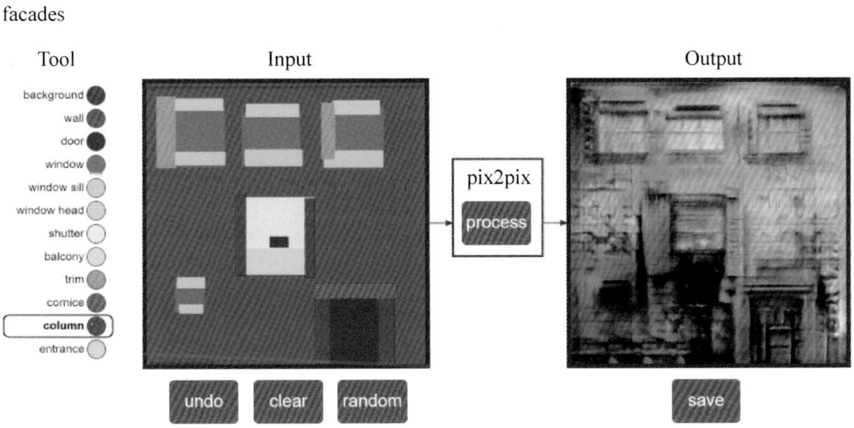

facades

Tool   Input   Output

图 4.4 pix2pix 模型网页 demo

图 4.21　界面展示图

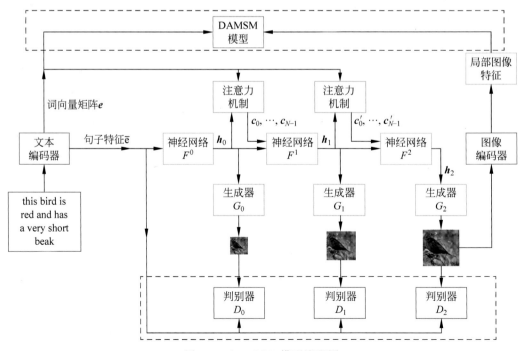

图 5.5　AttnGAN 模型流程图

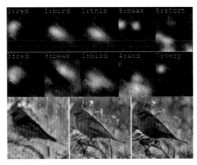

(a) this bird is red and has a very short beak　　　(b) this bird has a green crown black primaries and a white belly

图 5.8　实验结果图

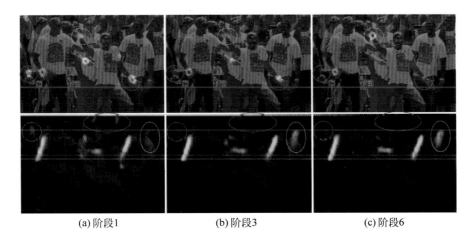

(a) 阶段1　　　　　　　(b) 阶段3　　　　　　　(c) 阶段6

图 6.7　跨阶段右前臂的右手腕(第一行)的置信度图和 PAF(第二行)

(a) 检测的身体关节　　　(b) 错误的关联　　　(c) 消除错误关联

图 6.9　关节关联策略

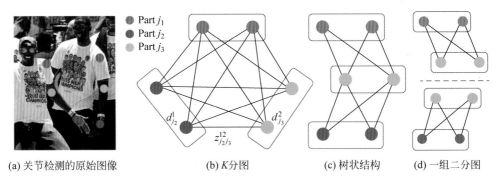

(a) 关节检测的原始图像　　(b) K分图　　(c) 树状结构　　(d) 一组二分图

图 6.11　图匹配

(a) 多姿态估计

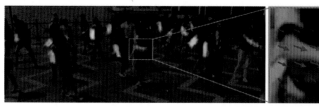

(b) PAFs   (c) 放大后的PAFs

图 6.13　局部网络示意图

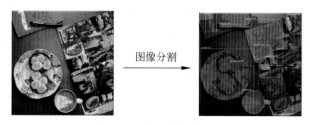

图 7.1　图像分割任务

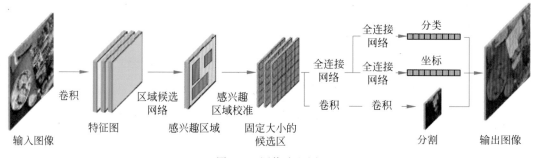

图 7.6　网络流程图

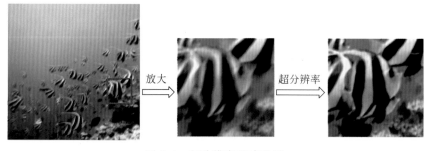

图 8.4　超分辨率重建效果

图 10.1　JDAI-Face 检测结果

图 11.8　数据集部分图像展示

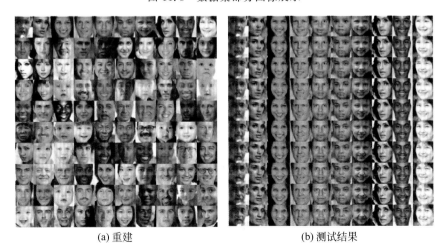

(a) 重建　　　　　　　　　　　　　　　(b) 测试结果

图 11.9　训练得到的图像展示

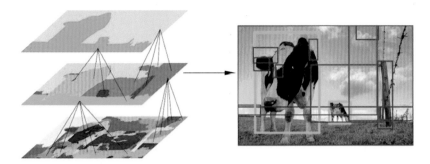

图 12.9 选择性搜索示意图(来源:简书)

图 12.10 左为锚框示意图,右为概率较大的锚框

(来源:https://ss0.baidu.com/6ON1bjeh1 BF3odCf/it/u=303494389,1516259513&fm=15&gp=0.jpg)

(a) 非极大值抑制前

(b) 非极大值抑制后

图 12.11 非极大值抑制前后比较

(来源:https://encrypted-tbn0.gstatic.com/images?q=tbn%3AANd9GcT6pkepYm

Wa0EgxqqE-XQ2pMYJOvaGqx4H3wA&usqp=CAU)

图 12.17　Demo 测试输出图

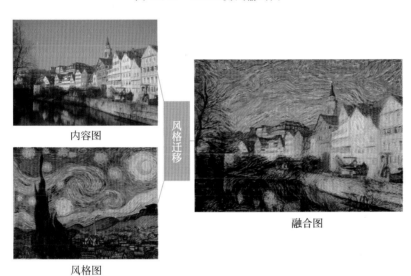

内容图

风格
迁移

融合图

风格图

图 17.2　将《星空》的风格迁移到建筑物图片(Gatys et al,2016)

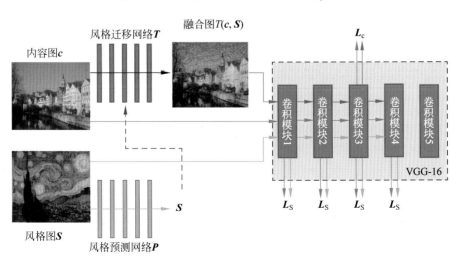

图 17.3　图像风格化模型

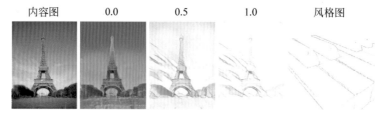

图 17.10　生成不同风格化程度的融合图

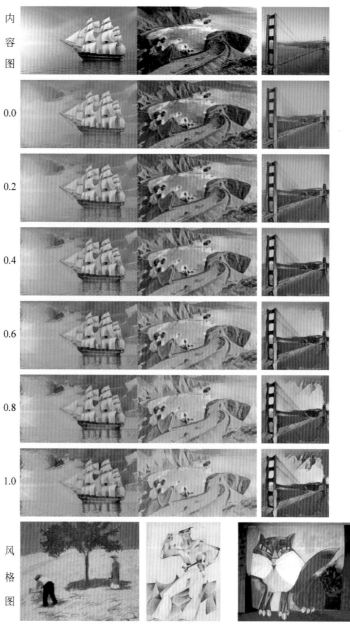

图 17.12　不同风格化程度的融合图